D1604747

Disney

Tim Burton's
THE NIGHTMARE BEFORE CHRISTMAS

Disney

Tim Burton's THE NIGHTMARE BEFORE CHRISTMAS

BEYOND HALLOWEEN TOWN

THE STORY + THE CHARACTERS + THE LEGACY

Emily Zemler
Foreword by Tim Burton

First published in 2023 by Epic Ink,
an imprint of The Quarto Group,
142 West 36th Street, 4th Floor,
New York, NY 10018, USA
T (212) 779-4972 F (212) 779-6058
www.Quarto.com

Epic Ink titles are also available at discount for retail, wholesale, promotional, and bulk purchase.
For details, contact the Special Sales Manager by email at specialsales@quarto.com or by mail at
The Quarto Group, Attn: Special Sales Manager, 100 Cummings Center Suite 265D, Beverly, MA 01915 USA.

10 9 8 7 6 5 4 3 2 1

ISBN: 978-0-7603-8098-7

Library of Congress Cataloging-in-Publication Data

Names: Zemler, Emily, author.
Title: Disney Tim Burton's The nightmare before Christmas : beyond Halloween Town:
  the story, the characters, and the legacy / by Emily Zemler.
Other titles: Nightmare before Christmas
Description: New York, NY : Epic Ink, 2023. | Includes index. | Summary:
  "In celebration of the thirtieth anniversary in 2023, Disney Tim
  Burton's The Nightmare Before Christmas: Beyond Halloween Town explores
  the beloved movie's creation, journey into pop-culture phenomenon, and
  its legacy with original interviews, behind-the-scenes photos, and
  memorabilia"-- Provided by publisher.
Identifiers: LCCN 2022060003 (print) | LCCN 2022060004 (ebook) | ISBN
  9780760380987 (hardcover) | ISBN 9780760380994 (ebook)
Subjects: LCSH: Tim Burton's The nightmare before Christmas (Motion
  picture)
Classification: LCC PN1997.N522353 Z46 2023 (print) | LCC PN1997.N522353
  (ebook) | DDC 791.43/72--dc23/eng/20221227
LC record available at https://lccn.loc.gov/2022060003
LC ebook record available at https://lccn.loc.gov/2022060004

Group Publisher: Rage Kindelsperger
Creative Director: Laura Drew
Managing Editor: Cara Donaldson
Editor: Katie McGuire
Photo Research: Julie Alissi
Interior and Layout Design: Kim Winscher

Printed in China

CONTENTS

FOREWORD

THE STRANGE TALE OF
THE NIGHTMARE BEFORE CHRISTMAS . . .

BY TIM BURTON

In 1982, I wrote a poem entitled *The Nightmare Before Christmas*, influenced by my favorite children's author Dr. Seuss. At the time, I was working as an animator at Walt Disney Studios, making films such as *Vincent* and *Frankenweenie*, and was thinking maybe I should also adapt this poem into a short film or a television special. Like a lot of people, I grew up loving the animated specials like *Rudolph the Red-Nosed Reindeer* and *How the Grinch Stole Christmas*. I wanted to recreate something with the same kind of feeling that they gave me. Something to look forward to seeing every year.

I did a number of drawings, storyboards, and concept art and had Rick Heinrichs sculpt some character models, but I think Disney didn't get it and thought it was too weird or dark at the time, so it didn't happen. I left Disney a little bit after that and made some other films like *Pee-wee's Big Adventure*, *Beetlejuice*, and *Batman*, but I couldn't forget *Nightmare*—it's the one film I knew had to be made. Eventually Disney came around and I think saw this as an opportunity to do something different. I knew it had to be stop-motion animation. The first film I remember seeing in cinemas was *Jason and the Argonauts* and Ray Harryhausen's animation felt so mind-blowingly

real. The handmade tactile quality of stop-motion felt perfect for this story.

I was lucky to know Henry Selick from CalArts and Disney, a great artist who also didn't fit in at Disney and who at the time was working with people who also had a love of stop-motion. So with Henry and an amazing group of artists, we created our own stop-motion studio, and with a fairly low budget (for an animated film), took this old technique and made it feel new again. It took over three years to make. Disney released it under their Touchstone banner, as they felt it was too dark for Walt Disney Pictures. When released, it was deemed a minor success, but then the film took on a life of its own. That's when everything got weird.

Beyond the film, from Disney turning the Haunted Mansion into a *Nightmare Before Christmas* experience, to *Nightmare*-themed weddings, to Danny Elfman's amazing *Nightmare* concerts at Royal Albert Hall and the Hollywood Bowl, I feel incredibly touched by the *Nightmare* vibe.

I meet people who say their young children love it, even many who say their dogs like it! People show me their tattoos, their amazing costumes— the connection I feel from people is very special.

Thank you for your love for thirty years.

INTRODUCTION
THE LITTLE MOVIE THAT COULD

Growing up, I aspired to be a film director. Although I was too young to know the word "auteur," I instinctually understood the concept: a filmmaker with a singular, unique vision whose work shares connective themes and visual touchstones. One of the earliest books I read about filmmaking was *Burton on Burton*, a 1995 tome by Tim Burton himself. In its chapters, Burton recounted the inspirations behind many of his films, including his early obsession with stop-motion animation. By the time I read the director's musings in the late nineties, everyone knew what a Tim Burton movie looked like. There was a signature aesthetic that threaded through his work, along with a core message about feeling like an outcast and eventually learning to find a sense of belonging.

Tim Burton's The Nightmare Before Christmas, released in theaters in 1993, exemplified that signature style, even though Burton handed directorial duties over to Henry Selick due to his commitment to helm *Batman Returns* (1992). The story, based on a poem Burton wrote in the early eighties, was brought to life over two years with classic stop-motion animation. Its crew, a skilled group of artists working out of a warehouse in San Francisco, channeled Burton's original vision into an achievement in filmmaking that remains unparalleled. Disney Legend Danny Elfman, who wrote the musical numbers and score, and Caroline Thompson, the screenwriter, augmented the film's emotional heft. When it was released, however, *Nightmare* was only embraced by a

Below: Tim Burton's vision resulted in a unique, handcrafted film that has become a holiday classic; *Opposite:* Jack Skellington, the Pumpkin King of Halloween Town.

core group of Burton fans and failed to gain further momentum. It seemed to come and go.

But like all misfits, *Tim Burton's The Nightmare Before Christmas* eventually found its clan. Over the years, the film's audience grew and grew, and it became a cultural phenomenon unto itself. Its world and characters, from Jack Skellington to Sally to Oogie Boogie, continue to resonate with fans around the world and encourage viewers to find connection in unlikely places. *Nightmare* has inspired everything from weddings to cover songs to tattoos to fashion choices. Its story has continued on in video games, novels, and merchandise. There is a shared love of the film that transcends generations and cultural backgrounds. It unites those who may initially seem dissimilar, and it urges communal

celebrations at Halloween, Christmas, and every holiday in between.

Since the film was made, Burton has gone on to direct many more projects. But over the past three decades, it has remained one of his most personal movies. From sketch to screen to nostalgic memory, Jack Skellington has never left Burton's mind—or his heart.

"It was a film that came from inside, from my subconscious," Burton says. "It was percolating for many many years, so it's something that's stayed with me. In fact, it did take, from inception to start, ten years. I can't say that about a lot of things—relationships, projects, anything. Jack kept coming up and I always try to rely on the subconscious rather than the intellectual. I kept thinking, 'Why do I keep

Jack and Sally's love story has remained one of the film's most significant legacies.

Many viewers relate to Jack's journey of self-discovery in the film.

drawing this thing?' Probably because it was simple and easy to doodle. That's why I think, for me, the film stayed so deep. It was deep for me and there are not a lot of things that have that impact on me."

It's an impact Burton now shares with millions of fans. The whimsical world of Halloween Town and its misfit inhabitants have transcended the filmmaker's original concept to become something far greater. For me, as a black clothing-clad weirdo growing up amid a sea of Abercrombie-wearing popular kids, Burton's work was a mirror, reflecting how I saw myself. Others saw themselves in there, too, especially in Halloween Town. Today, the film lives on because of those devoted fans, who have carried it from cult classic into the mainstream. And

it offers something for all of us, whether you're a misfit or not.

Looking back, it's clear why *Tim Burton's The Nightmare Before Christmas* is so captivating. The skill and artistry it took to create the film is almost unbelievable. It's a masterpiece in animation history and an example of auteur filmmaking at its finest. When I first saw the film, on a battered VHS tape from Blockbuster, I remember thinking I'd never seen anything like it before. Thirty years later, that assertion remains true. What we each take away from the film is unique and personal, but there's a shared sense of hope and community within the dark, moonlit landscapes. No matter how difficult life gets, we'll always be able to come back to Halloween Town.

Welcome to Halloween Town

ORIGINS AND INSPIRATIONS

As with the film's growth into a wide-reaching pop culture phenomenon, the road to creating *Tim Burton's The Nightmare Before Christmas* was long and winding. It began with an idea that took hold in Burton's mind while he was hired as an animator and concept artist at Walt Disney Animation Studios in the 1980s after graduating from the California Institute of the Arts, also known as CalArts. During his tenure at Disney, the filmmaker worked on *The Fox and The Hound* (1981) and, later, on *The Black Cauldron* (1985), but the doe-eyed animals didn't suit his darker aesthetic. The director's debut short film, *Vincent* (1982), narrated by Vincent Price, better exemplified the sorts of movies he wanted to make and the types of characters who interested him. As he worked for the studio, Burton continued conceiving his own stories and imagining fantastical worlds that could be created onscreen.

A short time after completing *Vincent*, Burton wrote a poem about a character named Jack Skellington. The lyrical poem was inspired by Clement Clark Moore's iconic holiday verse "A Visit from St. Nicholas," more commonly known as "The Night Before Christmas." Moore's poem, originally published on December 23, 1832, recounted the magic of Santa Claus visiting children's homes on Christmas Eve. In Burton's reworked version, Jack, who hails from a land called Halloween Town, takes over Santa's job with his trusty canine pal Zero, but ultimately bungles the delivery of the Christmas presents. The poem iteration of Jack Skellington existed alongside a visual depiction of him as a gaunt, elegant skeleton, which Burton had been repeatedly sketching in his spare time.

"The Jack character just came out as a drawing," Burton remembers. "I was bored, so I would doodle things a lot. It was an image that kept coming up. I think it was about roughly the same time I wrote the poem, but it wasn't necessarily directly linked. It was one of those subconscious things. He was a character that I kept drawing and it was all percolating roughly at the same time."

The filmmaker had a lifelong love of Christmas and Halloween, two holidays he often merged into one in his own celebrations. In writing the poem, he was inspired as much by Moore's original as by Dr. Seuss, particularly the author's 1957 classic *How the Grinch Stole Christmas!*. "I grew up loving Dr. Seuss," the filmmaker noted. "The rhythm of his stuff spoke to me very clearly. Dr. Seuss's books were perfect: right number of words, the right rhythm, great subversive stories."

Originally, Burton intended to publish *The Nightmare Before Christmas* as a children's book. He recalls taking it to nearly every publisher in New York City around the same time he was working on *The Black Cauldron*. While the publishers were captivated by the story, every publishing house ultimately passed. "I truly went almost everywhere and no one wanted it," Burton says. "At the time, I loved it and I just wanted to get it published."

Below: Burton drew inspiration from past versions of the story of Santa Claus; *Right:* Dr. Seuss' iconic character The Grinch.

SANTA'S MIDNIGHT RIDE

Top: Jack and his friends prepare for Christmas;
Inset (left): Rick Heinrichs' original model of Jack;
Inset (right): Concept art for Jack's sleigh.

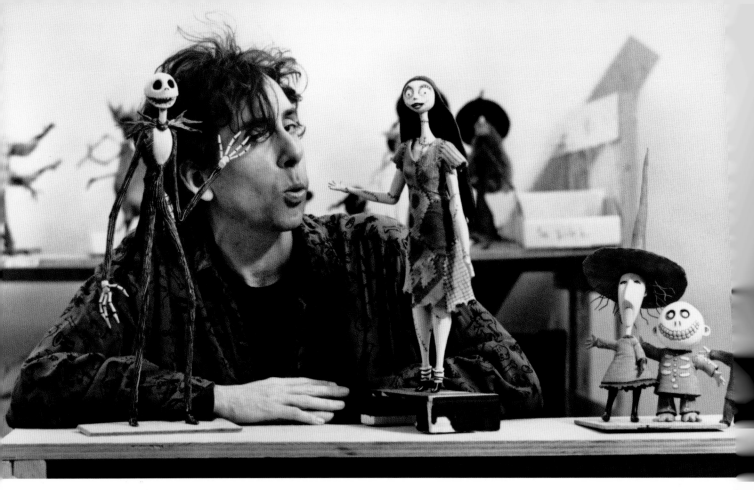

Tim Burton poses with models of Jack and Sally during the making of the film. To the right are Shock, Barrel, and Lock figures.

Undeterred, Burton shifted his focus to adapting the poem into a stop-motion holiday film similar to Rankin/Bass's *Rudolph the Red-Nosed Reindeer*, which first aired on television in 1964 and became an annual viewing tradition. He sketched concept artwork and storyboards expanding Jack's world, and enlisted model maker and production designer Rick Heinrichs, with whom he'd collaborated on *Vincent*, to create a 3D model of Jack. The pair pitched the film to The Walt Disney Company as a stop-motion animated feature that would evoke both Halloween and Christmas.

"Stop-motion had a power over me and reality to it that felt right for this story," Burton says. "That's why I held out for it, because it was the right way to go. I always knew it, even though at the early stages someone had suggested to make a half-hour film. In fact, they even suggested making it a drawn animated special. But I couldn't do that because Jack felt too real to me. To me, stop-motion had the emotion and the realism that fit this material. And that's why it took so long to get it made."

At the time, Burton put the idea aside with the intention of eventually revisiting Jack Skellington. "Everybody said they liked it, but not enough to do it at that time," the filmmaker said. "I guess that was my first real taste of that kind of show business mentality—a nice big smile and an 'Oh yeah, we're going to do this.' But, as you proceed, it becomes less and less of a reality."

THE PRODUCTION

The opportunity to bring Halloween Town to life finally came several years later, in 1990, when Burton inquired about the rights to the concept and discovered they were still owned by The Walt Disney Company. The studio agreed to let him make the film on his own terms, but the green light arrived at the same time that Burton was scheduled to direct *Batman Returns*, a sequel to his 1989 film *Batman*. Unwilling to pass up the opportunity, Burton tapped his old friend Henry Selick, a well-known stop-motion director who he met while the pair were students at CalArts, to step in and bring the holiday tale to life.

Although he felt very close to the story, Burton didn't hesitate when it came to handing over creative control.

"It was probably the only project that I've ever done where it felt very clear to me," Burton says. "It was very clear to me and that's why I felt comfortable with Henry and these artists and all the other people coming onboard. Stop-motion is such a long process. You have to plan it, and you have to do a lot of research to get the technical things right. But it was a strong group of people who were real artists, so I felt very comfortable about that for the only time in my life."

In July of 1991, Selick and a crew of one hundred and twenty began production on *Tim Burton's The Nightmare Before Christmas* at Skellington studio, a former warehouse in San Francisco's South of Market neighborhood. Selick drew on local talent, including animators, model makers, and set builders from George Lucas's nearby studio Industrial Light & Magic (ILM), as well as crew members from around the world, who

each brought their own inspirations to the table. Several came from *Gumby Adventures* (1988), a claymation TV series based on Art Clokey's iconic green character. This influx of international talent meant that *Nightmare*'s crew was comprised of the best of the best in their respective fields and ensured a diverse background of influences when it came to the realization of the film. Still, it was a daunting task. "Usually you do stop-motion for a one-minute

Below: Skellington studio in San Francisco; *Inset:* Director Henry Selick.

Top: Storyboards for a key scene in the film; *Inset (left):* Henry Selick and producer Kathleen Gavin in the studio; *Inset (right):* Oogie Boogie's model with concept sketches.

commercial," noted producer Denise Di Novi, who ran Tim Burton Productions at the time. "But we needed to build a whole studio from scratch. And we had to comb the world for animators."

Skellington studio was constructed from the ground up, with all of the film's departments working under one roof—something that is rare for a Hollywood movie production. Most of the crew was relatively young and there was a youthful, creative energy that ran through the studio. Several of them spent their evenings out at concerts in San Francisco and showed up to work on motorcycles. Some recall feeling like misfits and outcasts themselves, a connection to the film's story that resonated with those making it.

"A lot of us were young punks and listened to loud music and went out every night," recalls the film's production coordinator Kat Alioshin. "Here was this scary-looking, dark story. We reacted with, 'Oh, yes, we're gonna love working on this.' Because every other film seemed to be so happy and lighthearted, and this was an intense, coming-of-age story of Jack trying to figure out what he wanted to do with his life. We all related to him."

"We had a lot of fun," adds associate producer Phil Lofaro. "Everybody was pretty young. We had a lot of tattooed, pierced biker types. You know, it was San Francisco, and so it had an outlaw feel to it. And that was fun."

Production on the film lasted nearly two years. It was a constant process of trial and error, with many of the crew members innovating techniques to make the stop-motion better. It required seven hundred total shots—a huge number for a stop-motion animated feature—and it was an immense challenge that tested the skills of the crew members.

"There were a lot of problems to solve and there was no reference book to look up them up in," set builder Todd Lookinland explains. "We had to figure out, 'How are we going to do this?' That makes it a really fun environment because you have to get creative and figure it out, whether it's a camera technique or a material that you're going to use to build something or a painting technique. There was no handbook on this movie. We just made it all up as we went along."

"Each day was just a new way of trying to solve problems we hadn't confronted before," Lofaro notes. "That's what we did for two years—we solved problems. And ultimately, it produced the film that you see now."

The process of crafting a stop-motion feature is particularly arduous and requires an enormous amount of time, precision, and detail. Despite the

The filmmakers created models of the characters with removable clothing and faces.

intensity of the work, many of the crew look back on the experience as the best time of their career. From the model makers to the set builders to the animators to the storyboard artists, everyone was dedicated to bringing Burton's concept to life inside Skellington studio. Burton retained oversight over the project, sometimes visiting the studio in San Francisco to check on the progress. Heinrichs was brought on as visual consultant on the film to ensure continuity while simultaneously working as the production designer on *Batman Returns*. While a large crew came together to create the film, it was ultimately brought to life as a reflection of Burton's specific sensibility.

"It doesn't feel corporate," Heinrichs reflects on the process. "It doesn't feel like it went through committees, by any means. It feels very personal and I think that is a huge part of its success. It really does feel like a rather creative person came up with this world. While it actually was a team of people, everybody really was dedicated to giving Tim back the best version of what we could all do that aligned with his vision."

Below: Phil Brotherton and Todd Lookinland during set construction; *Inset:* Production notes for various shots.

SKELLINGTON PRODUCTIONS
CRYPT NOTES
DATE: FRIDAY, MAY 7, 1993

1302/8.1 (Take 1 & 2)	Approved take 1. Moves on to 406/1.
701/21 (Take 1)	Approved. Moves on to 701/23.
1201/4 (Take 1)	Approved. Moves on to 701/23.
1200/1 (Take 2)	Approved. Moves on to 1201/1.
400/6 (Take 1)	Approved. Moves on to 101/10.
403/5 (Take 1)	Approved. Moves on to 801/6. (REEL 2 IS FINITO.)
1400/11Z (Take 1)	FINAL APPROVAL TBD TOMORROW.
1301.2/11 (Test 4) Shoots today-tomorrow.	Camera/Lighting: Five x's will be added to shot after Mayor says, "...my boy." Soften edge of beam so it looks less artificial. Bring up spike a little. Props/Set: Texture part of floor. Mike: Animation per discussion w/ Henry.
801/17 (Test 2) Preps today. Shoots tomorrow-Monday.	Camera/Lighting: Pan about one field. Character: Sally's left elbow needs help. Anthony: Animation per discussion w/ Henry.
702/40 (Test 3) Preps today. Shoots tomorrow.	Camera/Lighting: Bring up firelight from below. Final position is too low; tilt up 1/2 field. Light newly placed clouds. Hit numbers without creating shadows on them. Bring up top of clocktower and wreath. Garland will be lit. Props/Set: Clean up clocktower face. Add clouds. Light up garland. Kim: Animation per discussion w/ Henry.
1301/10 (Test 6) Preps today-tomorrow. Shoots Monday-Tuesday.	Camera/Lighting: Blades may need help to read as metal. Use green gel. Props/Set: Blades need to read as blades immediately. Repo Oogie's lever. Paul: Animation per discussion w/ Henry.
1205/2 (Test 3) Preps today-Tuesday. Shoots Wednesday-Monday.	Camera/Lighting: More specialized light on Santa. (Check wedges.) Put the shadow of the mixer across Santa's undies. Overall dark. Pull back a little. Soup should be the brightest aspect of shot. Lever to platform needs to read after it's installed on set. Props/Set: Painted shadows need work; soften edges. Center mixing unit. Thicken soup goo mixture. Repo lever so it's within T.V. cut off (raise it up). Grease bottom of Sally/Santa platform. Lever to platform needs to be installed. Eric: Animation per discussion w/ Henry.
1000/4 (Test 3) Preps tomorrow-Tuesday. Shoots Wednesday-Friday.	Camera/Lighting: Get cam closer with wider lens so Jack and sled team don't look flat. Justin: (He'll animate.)
1206/19	Shoots through today.
1301.2/4	Shoots through tomorrow.
1400/11Z	Shoots through tomorrow.
900/4	Shoots through tomorrow.

Crew members Jo Carson and Jim Matlosz prepare a scene during the film's production.

THE STORY

Although *Tim Burton's The Nightmare Before Christmas* originated as a fairly lengthy and descriptive poem, Burton knew the story needed to be fleshed out in order to work as a feature-length film. The poem featured only three characters: Jack Skellington, Zero, and Santa Claus, and it didn't have the full character arc required of a movie narrative. Initially, Burton tapped *Beetlejuice* screenwriter Michael McDowell to adapt the poem into a script, but that collaboration ultimately didn't work out. The filmmaker instead pivoted to collaborating with Danny Elfman to make the film into a musical.

Alongside Burton, Elfman wrote several musical numbers, working from a story outline and a collection of sketches that detailed Jack's scheme to save Christmas after kidnapping Santa Claus. The pair drew on various influences, including Burton's long-held feelings of being a misfit and Elfman's personal experiences as the beloved leader of a rock band, Oingo Boingo, which he wanted to leave. Burton also pulled inspiration from the monster movies he'd loved as a child when imaging Jack, an unlikely hero.

"He's the classic misunderstood monster," Burton explains. "I grew up watching monster movies and I felt all monsters were actually not villains but the most emotional characters in the films, like Frankenstein and King Kong. Every monster is perceived as the bad guy, but they're not that bad of a guy. They're tortured, they're misguided, but they're not bad people. Feeling how I did about Halloween and Christmas, with a certain opposite juxtaposition of those holidays, the story and the character came together based on a lot of feelings that I had about a lot of things. Jack was always very positive, very energetic, and very misguided. Jack is an optimistic character. He's something that's perceived as scary or bad, but he is truly just a good person and a positive, artistic person. That's why I always loved Ed Wood, because it was like, 'He's horrible, but passionate and cares about something even if it's garbage.' I've always identified with those types of characters."

When production began on the film in July of 1991, there was no actual screenplay. The filmmakers had shot some test footage at visual effects supervisor Phil Tippett's studio in Berkeley, but once they moved into the San Francisco studio the work needed to begin in earnest. Selick and his crew started animating one of the songs, which Elfman had recorded as a demo, using storyboards by artist Joe Ranft for reference, to ensure there was no delay in the production. They purposefully selected the most colorful, whimsical musical sequence to encourage more support from The Walt Disney Company and its offshoot Touchstone Pictures, which would distribute the film.

"Danny knew there had to be a scene where Jack Skellington discovers Christmas Town, so he wrote and recorded 'What's This?,'" cinematographer Pete Kozachik explained. "That got us going. Joe Ranft and his guys churned out storyboards to illustrate the song, which fed production designer Deane Taylor and his assistants. Henry picked one shot out of the thirty-six shots boarded, shot number WHA-32. That would be the shot we'd begin the movie with."

Despite the success of the initial sequence, which took weeks to shoot, the filmmakers knew they needed a script as soon as possible. While Elfman was writing the songs he was living with then-partner Caroline Thompson, the screenwriter of Burton's *Edward Scissorhands,* who became instrumental in shaping the characters and narrative of *Tim Burton's The Nightmare Before Christmas.* Because Thompson was already familiar with the overall story and the characters, the studio asked if she would come on board to write the script at the same time production was kicking off. It was a somewhat backwards process.

"Danny had really told the whole story in song," Thompson remembers. "If you pull the songs out, they tell an entire tale. So I said, 'Well,

I'll think about it.' Sally had to be redesigned for me to come in, and a couple of images came to me. One was her throwing herself out of the tower, and because she was stitched together, it gave me like a Frankenstein image. I saw all of her limbs falling and then I saw her back together again. The other image that came to me was her detaching her leg and leaving it for Oogie Boogie while she went to free Santa on the other side of the cave. Having those two images, I was comfortable saying, 'Okay, I'll take a crack at it."

Thompson went to visit the animators and crew at Skellington studio, where she saw dozens of sketches and storyboards. Her goal was to flesh out the characters and to create a story arc that existed outside of Elfman's songs. After seeing a sketch of the Evil Scientist, who is also known as Dr. Finkelstein, removing his head and scratching his brain, she had the idea to create a subplot about the scientist as Sally's creator and Sally's eventual plan to escape him. Following her visit to the studio,

Screenwriter Caroline Thompson.

Sally's look evolved dramatically, from femme fatale to kind-hearted rag doll.

Thompson and Elfman took a trip to a resort in Northern California where she wrote the screenplay in a week. The first draft of the script, dated August 5, 1991, was the only draft. It arrived just in time.

"Caroline is a talented writer and sort of pieced things together as Danny continued writing great songs," Selick remembers. "There are definitely some rose-colored glasses looking backward at all this. It wasn't easy. But I really think it was just fun and blind faith that kept us going, so we never got too down. As we went along, I was so interested in finding out about Jack and who he was. There was a sweetness and an insanity to him that I loved. You wanted to be carried along with the story. At the end of the day, the film is about that character and instantly connecting with him and wanting to see how things are going to work out."

Alongside Thompson's screenplay and Elfman's songs, Selick and his crew took inspiration from a number of sources, both thematically and visually. Earlier films like Czech surrealist animator Jan Švankmajer's 1971 work *Jabberwocky* and Roy Rowland's 1953 film *The 5,000 Fingers of Dr. T.*, based on a story by Dr. Seuss, impacted the storytelling. Other influences included Charles Laughton's *The Night of the Hunter* (1955), Terry Gilliam's *The Adventures of Baron Munchausen* (1988), and Robert Wiene's *The Cabinet of Dr. Caligari* (1920).

"I've always said that Tim and I are from the same planet, just not the same neighborhood," Selick recalls. "So I was building a style based on my inspirations, which included Tim. We drew much more from live-action films and illustrators and artists and so forth because there just weren't that many stop-motion films done in the style that we were going to be working in."

Although the film came to fruition in an unusual way, with the story and the songs being crafted before the actual script, the result is a compelling tale about two misfits who find belonging and, eventually, love. It reflects the inspirations of both Thompson and Elfman, whose contributions came together to create Sally and Jack. Although Jack is the protagonist, the emotional heft of the story relies on Sally as well.

"I'm proud that I was able to knit some coherence into something that could have really gone south," Thompson says. "I was able to find a supporting story to carry the narrative. Sally's story carries the movie in terms of narrative and Jack's story carries the movie in terms of song. And Sally accomplishes a great thing. She humanizes Jack. She gives him a dimension he didn't otherwise have and humanizes him."

The poster for 1953 film *The 5,000 Fingers of Dr. T.*

THE CHARACTERS

What's a fantastical world without vibrant, compelling inhabitants? Burton's original poem centered on only three characters: Jack Skellington, his pet dog Zero, and a specific iteration of Santa Claus. To translate the poem to the big screen, the filmmakers needed to populate Halloween Town with lively and sometimes horrific characters, from Sally to Oogie Boogie to the town's two-faced Mayor. As Jack discovers his purpose on a journey from Halloween Town to Christmas Town and back again, he encounters friends, foes, and family along the way. Despite their horrific appearances, none of the characters in *Tim Burton's The Nightmare Before Christmas* are intended to be evil. Instead, they highlight our common misconceptions about those who appear to be misfits.

"Here you have this story where there are no *really* bad characters, not even Oogie Boogie," Burton explained. "He's not really bad, he's just the weird neighbor in this weird city. And you have this character, Jack, who just wants to do good; he's passionate about something, and basically he ends up being misperceived and scaring everybody."

Top: A still from *The Cabinet of Dr. Caligari; Above:* A sketch of Jack and Sally.

Rick Heinrichs and the creative team
created concepts for the inhabitants of
Halloween Town, including a witch and
a melting man.

PUMPKIN KING

JORGEN —
YES! MUCH BETTER DESIGN.
MY SUGGESTION IS TO
MAKE HIM BURSTING
OUT OF HIS SHIRT.
SEE WHAT YOU THINK.
— RICK

Smallest Hyde pops up
from behind hat

Smallest Hyde pops up
from behind hat

While the film centers on several lead characters, with Jack at the forefront of the story, the filmmakers and animators needed to fill the story with background characters who matched Burton's original vision. Heinrichs and the art department looked at Burton's sketches and drawings for inspiration, but also conceived characters who felt right for the film's terrifying but endearing aesthetic.

"In the town meeting you see a lot of incidental characters, so we had to come up with ideas for that," Heinrichs remembers. "The witches and the vampires and the little kid with a sewn-up eye. There was a melting man—that was Tim's concept. I did a sculpture of him using wax that was really melting."

The vampires, in particular, have become a fan favorite. In the film, four caped vampires appear, each with his own personality and body shape. Heinrichs pulled from one of Burton's sketches to create the bloodsuckers.

"The vampires appear only briefly and have funny-sounding, high voices," Heinrichs says. "There was something about the way Tim depicted them that felt more real as a vampire than almost any other screen version of them. He somehow caught both the human and the animal quality, and it was funny at the same time. That's what Tim brings to all of his depictions of character by walking the line between the horror and humor—there's something that feels very organic to the character's essence in what he draws."

Each character had to be designed and built by the crew to help them feel as real as possible. Because the film was stop-motion, the characters were constructed as puppets with armature skeletons that allowed them to be moved millimeter by millimeter to create the sense of movement. Once they were built, they were decorated, painted, and dressed in costume. Several of the characters, including Jack and Sally, had removable heads or faces to allow them to change expression. After that, it was up to the animators to make each one feel alive onscreen, matching the motion and gestures to the voice cast's recordings. It was an involved process that ultimately allowed each character in the film to feel like a living, breathing person—or creature—who has a backstory and hopes for the future.

As the film's protagonist, Jack searches for meaning in his life.

Jack Skellington

Jack Skellington, the Pumpkin King of Halloween Town, is a dapper, energetic figure who is also grappling with some deep existential questions. He is disheartened by the same Halloween celebrations year after year, and he assumes that adventure will be found away from his community of Halloween Town.

"Jack is like a lot of characters in classic literature that are passionate and have a desire to do something in a way that isn't really acknowledged, just like that Don Quixote story, in which some character is on a quest for some sort of feeling, not even knowing what that is," Burton said. "It's a very primal thing to me, that kind of searching for something and not even knowing what it is, but being passionate about it. There are just aspects to the character of Jack that I like and identify with. It means something to me."

The character was also inspired by Elfman, who was the lead singer of Oingo Boingo at the time. "Jack was an extension of what I was feeling at the time," Elfman explained. "A lead singer in a band is like a king of their own little world, but I was at the point where I didn't want to be in a band anymore. I was writing from my own heart. He's got all these fans and people love him, but he's not happy."

Visually, Jack is based on Burton's early drawings of the character, which included the skeleton's bat-shaped bow tie. "Tim puts down his idea and pretty much doesn't change it," says Heinrichs, who sculpted the first 3D model of Jack. "But I was told by one of the armature builders that the legs were too skinny for them to build a practical joint within—Tim had just used a pen line for the legs and it was very thin. It was interesting to engage in that dialogue of the aesthetic versus the practical. Because stop-motion is all about what's practical in order to create the magical effect of it. It's real objects in real life, and Jack has an enormous amount of charm because of all the life the animators put into him."

While Elfman recorded Jack's musical numbers, actor Chris Sarandon was cast as his speaking voice, which is confident and has a specific rhythmic cadence. "There was a very clear pathway into the sound of the character both from hearing Danny singing and also from the visuals that I was provided," Sarandon remembers. "I recall Henry Selick and I talked about it a bit, but then we jumped right into it. We didn't talk deeply about the character because Jack's journey and how you have to get there are built into the script. And then we tried everything. It was very creative because I was allowed all sorts of choices reading the lines."

Sally

For many viewers, Sally, voiced by actress Catherine O'Hara, is the heart of the film. The character went through several iterations before the filmmakers landed on her rag doll design, which draws inspiration from Mary Shelley's 1818 novel *Frankenstein*, L. Frank Baum's 1913 novel *The Patchwork Girl of Oz*, and Catwoman, one of the villains in *Batman Returns*. Initially, Sally was drawn as a "sexy Bride of Frankenstein," according Heinrichs, but when Thompson stepped in the screenwriter wanted to ensure that Sally had the right aesthetic for the story. "I saw the image of Sally and said, 'I can't write about that,'" Thompson explains. "I said, 'You need to make her the Little Match Girl for me to be able to understand her.'"

Thompson also pulled from her own life as she created Sally. "The Sally character has the ability to look after herself and plots and plans and an understanding that nobody's gonna do it for her," Thompson noted. "So, that would have been me at that time."

The look of Catwoman, as played by Michelle Pfeiffer, featured a stitched-together leather costume, which inspired Sally's imagery. It was also intended as a visual reflection of her internal circumstances. "I was into stitching from the Catwoman thing, I was into that whole psychological thing of being pieced together," Burton explained of the way Sally is sewn together. "Again, these are all symbols for the way that you feel. The feeling of not being together

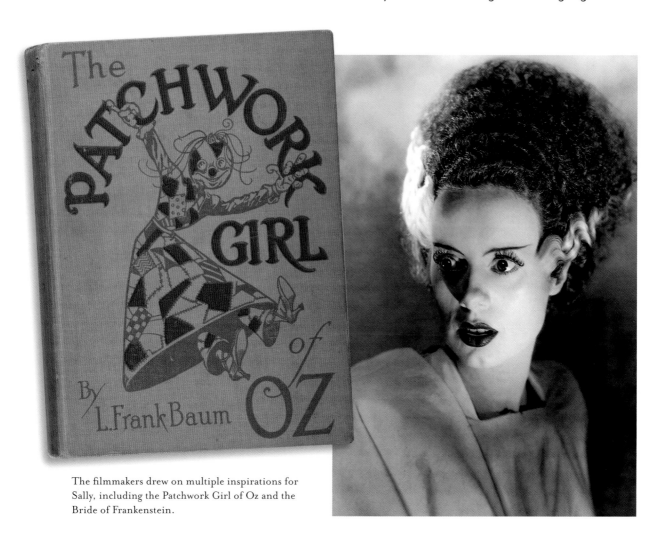

The filmmakers drew on multiple inspirations for Sally, including the Patchwork Girl of Oz and the Bride of Frankenstein.

Top: Sally with her many faces; *Inset:* Voice actress Catherine O'Hara.

and of being loosely stitched together and constantly trying to pull yourself together, so to speak, is just a strong feeling to me. So those kind of visual symbols have less to do with being based on *Frankenstein*, than with the feeling of pulling yourself together."

While Sally was inspired by the more homely character of the Little Match Girl, the filmmakers also wanted her to have an undeniable allure. "I wanted to push whatever glamour the Sally puppet had to offer," explained Kozachik. "We had a close-up of her just before she jumps out the window, and we studied glam photos from movies made in the 1930s and '40s and applied them to that little plastic head. Sally held her ground with the likes of Marlene Dietrich."

For O'Hara, it was a process of trial and error to discover Sally's voice. "I had many recording sessions with Henry in which he directed my dialogue almost a word at a time," she remembers. "It didn't feel easy or organic but it

was right for Sally. She's a man-made patchwork being who's still learning how to use her body and her voice."

She adds, "I didn't know Sally would affect people the way she has. She's not quite finished and doesn't know who she is and I guess many of us feel that way. She is in love, but until the end she believes her love might remain unrequited."

Stop-Motion Inspiration

Historically, the origins of stop-motion predate Hollywood and the advent of cinema. The animation technique, which uses individually photographed frames to create the illusion of movement, is rooted in photographic practices from the mid-nineteenth century and eventually filmmakers in the early twentieth century began experimenting with the art form. It's never been a prevalent style in Hollywood, but it's always been one that inspires Burton, who first encountered stop-motion animation in his childhood.

"There's an energy with stop-motion that you can't even describe," Burton noted. "It's to do with giving things life, and I guess that's why I wanted to get into animation originally. To give life to something that doesn't have it is cool, and even more so in three dimensions, because, at least for me, it feels even more real."

There have been numerous stop-motion shorts and features, as well as TV series and commercials, created since the form's inception, but a few specific films particularly inspired *Tim Burton's The Nightmare Before Christmas*. Both Burton and his collaborators drew on animation history for visual and thematic references. Some of the influences are more overt than others, but there were five films that notably impacted the creation of Halloween Town and its inhabitants.

The Cameraman's Revenge (1912)

An early example of stop-motion animation is filmmaker Ladislas Starevich's short *The Cameraman's Revenge*, which Heinrichs showed to the animators while making *Tim Burton's The Nightmare Before Christmas*. The film, about a love triangle, used actual dried insects as its stop-motion puppets in a monochrome setting.

The 7th Voyage of Sinbad (1958)

Stop-motion master Ray Harryhausen created numerous stop-motion films, including *The 7th Voyage of Sinbad*, a fantasy epic that is the first in a trilogy. While it was directed by Nathan H. Juran, the feature was conceptualized by Harryhausen, who had begun making stop-motion films in the 1950s. The story's fantastical creatures offered a starting point for Burton, who was also compelled by unlikely heroes and grotesque monsters.

Jason and the Argonauts (1963)

Harryhausen collaborated with director Don Chaffey for a retelling of the Greek myth of Jason, which was released in movie theaters in 1963. This particular Harryhausen effort left a mark on Burton when he saw it as a kid. "It was strong and goes right inside you and sticks with you like a dream," Burton reflected of the film. "Harryhausen was always a singular artist. It was like he was an actor; he was like the character. There was a personal feeling about the medium and the way he sort of infused it that made it a strong, visceral experience. The way all the monsters died, there was just a real sense of emotion in there that was really interesting."

Rudolph the Red-Nosed Reindeer (1964)

Produced by Rankin/Bass Productions, *Rudolph the Red-Nosed Reindeer* was based on Johnny Marks' holiday song "Rudolph the Red-Nosed Reindeer" and directed by Larry Roemer. It first aired on NBC, and has since become a seminal television event leading up to Christmas. It was filmed with a stop-motion animation process known as "Animagic" using small puppets, a few of which can still be found on the shelves of die-hard collectors. "Those crude stop-motion animation holiday things that were on year in, year out make an impact on you early and stay with you," Burton noted. "I had grown up with those and had a real feeling for them, and I think, without being too direct, the impulse was to do something like that."

Mad Monster Party? (1967)

While *Tim Burton's The Nightmare Before Christmas* is sometimes credited as the first stop-motion animated feature musical film, Jules Bass's *Mad Monster Party?* actually has that distinction. Also produced by Rankin/Bass Productions, the horror spoof featured the voices of Boris Karloff and Phyllis Diller and acquired the status of cult classic over the decades. The animated feature, intended for children, tells the story of Baron Boris von Frankenstein, living on the Isle of Evil, as he summons the world's most famous monsters with his messenger bats. Burton has professed his admiration for the film, which he watched as a child. "People thought *Nightmare* was the first stop-motion animated monster musical, but that was," Burton noted of *Mad Monster Party?*.

Oogie Boogie

Although Oogie Boogie is the primary villain of the film, the ghastly character didn't appear in Burton's original poem. Burton later sketched Oogie as a sinister sack-like being filled with creepy, crawly bugs, but it took some finessing to give him the right personality. The character was also a challenge for the animators, who used a two-foot puppet to literally flesh out the stop-motion character. Although he is the antagonist, Oogie Boogie purposefully veers between overtly sinister and hilariously grotesque.

Elfman drew inspiration from Cab Calloway's bluesy song and dance numbers in Betty Boop cartoons of the 1930s, including "Minnie the Moocher," as well as Calloway's own famous song "St. James Infirmary," for "Oogie Boogie's Song." Broadway actor Ken Page, who was enlisted to

Oogie Boogie had several inspirations, including (top to bottom) Bert Lahr, Mercedes McCambridge, and Cab Calloway.

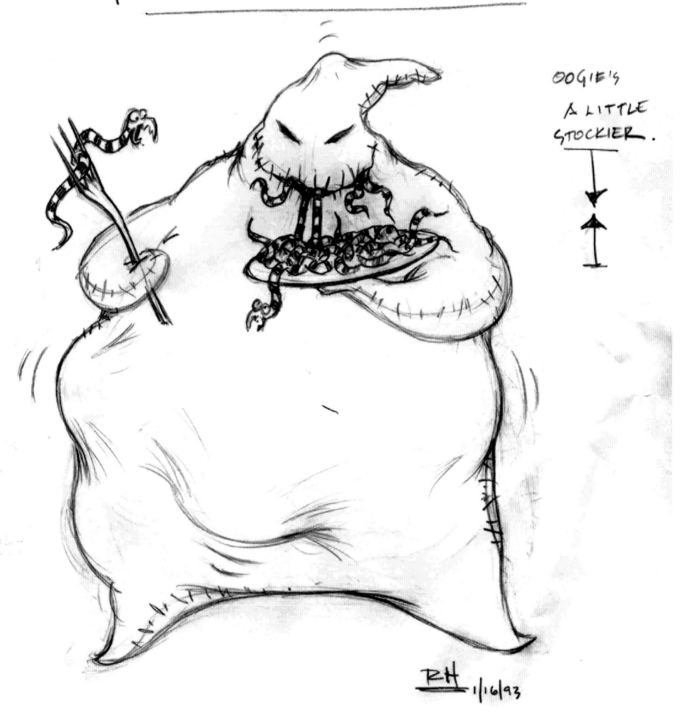

DON'T HAVE TOO MANY "STRAIGHT" SNAKES GOING INTO HIS MOUTH (IT'S HARD TO DECIPHER WHAT THEY ARE)

OOGIE'S A LITTLE STOCKIER.

RH 1/16/93

A development sketch of Oogie Boogie by Rick Heinrichs.

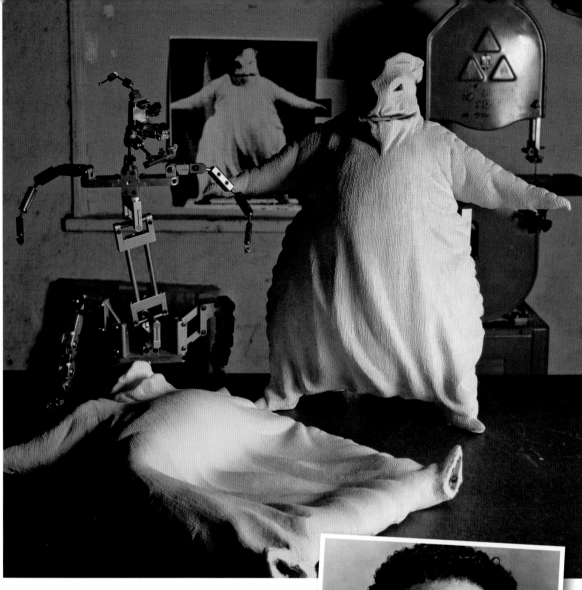

Top: Oogie Boogie with his armature (seen on the left);
Inset: Voice actor Ken Page.

voice Oogie Boogie, similarly looked to Hollywood history to find the best speaking voice for the villain. Page ended up combining two specific influences: Bert Lahr as the Cowardly Lion in *The Wizard of Oz* (1939) and Mercedes McCambridge as the demon in *The Exorcist* (1973).

"They were going, 'Oh, okay, wow, you're as weird as we are,'" Page remembers of the filmmakers' reaction to his artistic choice. "That was where I went with it. And it's me, of course, overlaid on all of it—my ethnicity and so on. Mercedes McCambridge's work in *The Exorcist*, to me, is probably the best voiceover work of all time. A lot of what affected us psychologically was her voice. Thinking about voicing a character that was going to be animated, I wanted to try to imbue it with as much of that same depth of character, even though you weren't seeing me.

I thought, 'If she could do that and scare the bejesus out of everybody, if I get anywhere near there I'm doing well.' But you didn't want to scare people completely and totally, so that was the the addition of Bert Lahr—lovable but still bigger than life. And, of course, I added my own hot sauce to it."

Evil Scientist

The Evil Scientist, Sally's inventor, feels familiar and unique at the same time. The character, voiced by actor William Hickey and sometimes known to fans as Dr. Finkelstein, draws an obvious inspiration from Victor Frankenstein. But the wheelchair-bound character also emerged from Burton's love of a genre he calls "brain movies," such as *The Brain from Planet Arous* (1957), *The Trollenberg Terror* (1958), and *Fiend Without a Face* (1958). "He goes back to my love of any kind of horror movie and the symbols and images and types that come from any of those movies," Burton notes.

The doctor has a hunchbacked sidekick, Igor, who is part of a long line of grotesque lab assistants aiding deranged scientists onscreen, notably in the 1958 horror flick *The Revenge of Frankenstein* and Mel Brooks' *Young Frankenstein* (1974). The Evil Scientist controls Sally and

Top right: Voice actor William Hickey; *Right:* Evil Scientist; *Below:* A still from *The Bride of Frankenstein*.

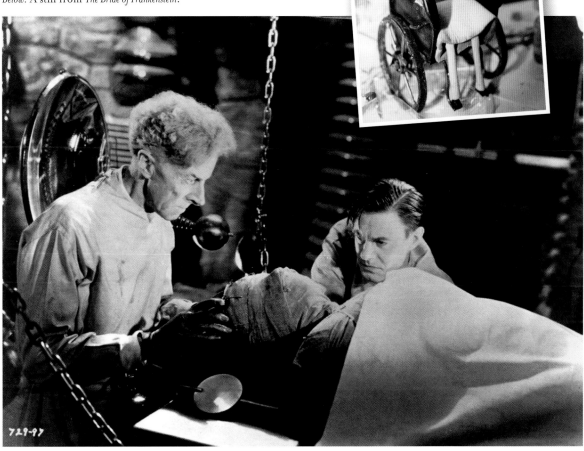

has some villainous tendencies, but Thompson intended him to be equal parts horrible and lovable.

"Early on, I saw a drawing that someone had done—it was of a scientist in a wheelchair with his head off, scrambling his own brains," Thompson recalled. "I thought it was charming. And I wanted Sally to have an obstacle between her and Jack that was visible as opposed to emotional. So I folded the Evil Scientist into the subplot."

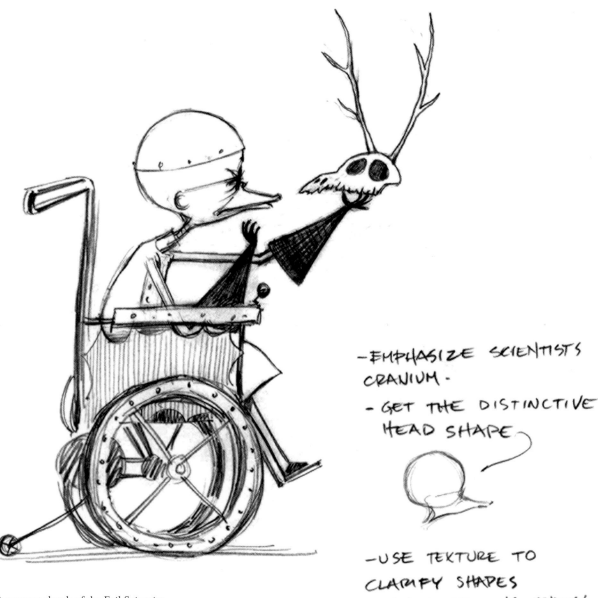

A concept sketch of the Evil Scientist.

-EMPHASIZE SCIENTISTS CRANIUM -
- GET THE DISTINCTIVE HEAD SHAPE

-USE TEXTURE TO CLARIFY SHAPES
- AVOID SHADING UNLESS YOU'RE REALLY DEFINING A SHAPE.

- GOOD LUCK !

RICK 10/13

Santa Claus

Santa Claus is a historical figure and literary character, but the incarnation in Burton's film, who is also known as Sandy Claws and was voiced by Ed Ivory, is purposefully less jolly. "There this juxtaposition of how Halloween is scary and Christmas is perceived as good and cheerful," the filmmaker explains. "But Santa Claus always scared me a little bit. Around Halloween you've been watching scary movies and monsters and then Christmas comes along and you're supposed to feel happy about this big, fat guy coming down your chimney on Christmas Eve. It's like a horror movie. So with Santa I didn't want to make him a bad person—he's just kind of weird. We kept what Santa is meant to represent, but with an off-kilter quality to him."

That edginess comes through in Santa's visual design, which retains his signature elements, like a red suit and hat, but adds an angular sensibility. "Everything was very shape-based," Heinrichs explains of designing Santa. "So as I was doing the sculptures, Santa Claus was a huge, very fat, circular funnel shape with his head and his hat and his beard. And he had no legs. He basically was a big, round cloak that went down to the floor. You do get to see his legs, but only in a few shots. That says something about *The Nightmare Before Christmas* and its handmade quality: A lot of things were specialty items that were made just for a specific shot. And in your mind that becomes a whole character, like, 'Oh, Santa has got legs.' He lives in our minds as a complete character because of those shots."

The film takes a unique spin on Santa Claus.

Zero

Jack Skellington's ghostly sidekick is, in typical
Burton style, a trusty dog. Zero evoked several
of Burton's own canine companions, as well as the
character of Sparky in his short film *Frankenweenie*.
The ghost pup is one of only three characters in
the film who appeared in Burton's original poem,
where the filmmaker described him as "the best
friend that Jack had ever had."

   "I had a few dogs when I was a child that were
very special to me," Burton says. "They were a
little heart that comes to life, so that was always
something that had a power to me. It was a bond
and a friendship and a feeling—a boy and his dog
thing that was very important to me. I've always
been lucky to have breeds that are a mixture and
I've had a couple of dogs that had an eccentricity
and specialness to them."

Top: While Rudolph has a shiny red nose, Zero has a tiny jack-o'-lantern; *Above:* Zero was inspired by Burton's own dogs.

Above: Voice actor Frank Welker; *Right:* A sculpt of Zero.

Zero, who eventually leads Jack's sleigh, has an obvious connection with Rudolph, the reindeer who guides Santa's sleigh. The only difference is that instead of a glowing red nose, Zero has a tiny jack-o'-lantern, which appeared in Burton's original drawings of the character.

Because Zero is a ghost, his body is fluid as he floats beside Jack. He's also translucent, which was a challenge for the filmmakers, who wanted to create the character practically, rather than using computer-generated visual effects in post-production.

"Zero would always be a see-through ghost, enabling us to use simple in-camera effects," explained Kozachik. "I enjoyed the dog shots as individual puzzles to be worked out. Most shots allowed us to simply wind back the film after animating Jack and then animate Zero against a black-velvet background. We put a strong fog-effect filter on the lens anytime we filmed Zero, giving him that ghostly look."

Lock, Shock, and Barrel

Lock, Shock, and Barrel are Halloween Town's most mischievous residents. Also known as Boogie's Boys, the trio plot and scheme to kidnap Santa Claus and deliver him to Oogie Boogie. They appear to be young trick-or-treaters—Lock wears a devil costume, Shock is dressed as a witch, and Barrel dons a skeleton outfit—and they share a clubhouse. For Burton, the inspiration behind the trio was simple. "They are just the horrible little kids we all know or had," Burton says. "I have a couple—No, they're not that bad. The sort of kids we all grew up with."

The filmmaker tapped three of his regular collaborators to voice the pesky children, who have a shared musical number, "Kidnap the Sandy Claws." Elfman performed Barrel, while O'Hara did double duty as Shock. For Lock, however, Burton wanted to nod to his directorial debut. He asked Paul Reubens, who he had worked with on *Pee-wee's Big Adventure* (1985), to play Lock. The idea was to evoke Reubens' signature character while keeping the character true to the story.

"He wanted the voice to be like Pee-wee," Reubens remembers. "When you do voice work you don't have the same tools you have as an actor—you're a voice actor—so it's really all about your voice. You have to put in as many colors and as many levels as you can. I'm proud of the work I did on it."

"I loved the experience of giving voices to Sally and Shock and I loved recording the songs," O'Hara adds. "One never really knows if their work will find an audience, but audiences just keep finding this movie."

A sketch of Lock, Shock, and Barrel.

The Mayor

The Mayor of Halloween Town is literally two-faced—
an apt visual metaphor for how politicians say
one thing and do another. The initial idea for the
double visage came from a drawing by one of
the artists, which Heinrichs refined through a
back-and-forth with Burton. The character was
voiced by Glenn Shadix, who also appeared in
Beetlejuice as Otho. As the leader of Halloween
Town, The Mayor drives a hearse, which was
designed by the film's art director Deane Taylor.
It was the first sketch Taylor did when he came on
board the film, and the car set the design standard
for much of what came after.

"I made it ridiculously long, with tiny little
wheels," Taylor says. "Which turned out to be a bit
problematic because it couldn't actually drive on
a lot of the roads. But that first-time rough sketch
felt like the solution to all these design questions
I had. I wanted to retain the spirit of that design
all the way through."

Head flips around to reveal
sad face and candy cane hat

Top: Voice actor Glenn Shadix; *Above:* The Mayor's dual faces.

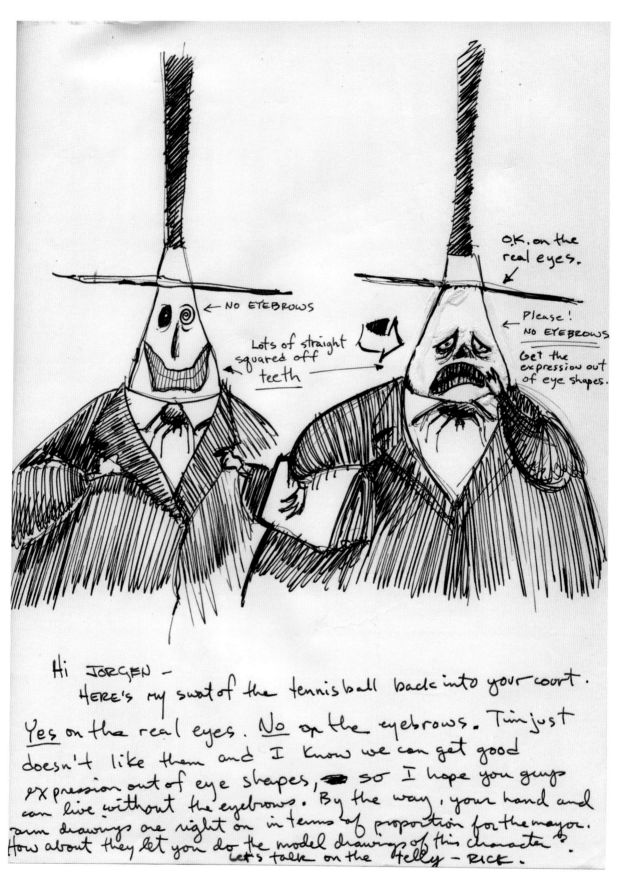

Concept art by Rick Heinrichs.

THE WORLD

In *Tim Burton's The Nightmare Before Christmas*, Jack Skellington discovers a circle of magical trees, each of which has a doorway to a holiday world. Although the story is largely set in Halloween Town, the scope of the narrative is much broader, transporting Jack to Christmas Town, as well as into the real world, where children await the arrival of Santa Claus. Each set piece was designed and constructed from scratch by the film's crew, often using sketches created by Burton. The filmmakers drew on numerous inspirations for each location, including German Expressionism, Dr. Seuss, Edward Gorey, Charles Addams, and Francis Bacon. Many of the sets were based on Burton's sketches, but art director Deane Taylor and his team were heavily involved in the concepts, as was Rick Heinrichs. The artists interpreted Burton's concepts and then sent them to be modeled, built, painted, and dressed by other members of the crew.

"Tim had this whole mountain of imagery that he had done for various projects that we all took onboard as an influence, so everything we did was steeped in the Tim Burton style," Heinrichs remembers. "Tim's influence can be seen in the simplicity of the shapes and in the strong colors and the use of primary colors. It's also in the development of the specific looks for the different worlds of Christmas Town, the real world, and Halloween Town."

Thanks to its specificity and careful design, the world of Halloween Town is memorable and feels incredibly real despite being a fantastical location. Each set in the film evokes a tangible setting that gives even more life to the story.

The filmmakers drew on numerous inspirations, including German Expressionism and Ronald Searle's artwork.

Halloween Town

Halloween Town, where most of the action takes place, is dark and visually compelling. It was rendered primarily in black, white, and orange—a directive from Burton—and the lines are intentionally angular and sharp. It was also intended to be entertainingly whimsical. "Halloween Town needed to be Gothic and have a sense of humor," Taylor recalls. "Like if you took Frankenstein and told Charles Addams to draw it like the Addams Family, you would get a Gothic humor. I thought that was important. Things like the front door of Jack's house where the doorbell was a spider that you had to pull on. I wanted to add touches of humor wherever we could."

German Expressionism was a huge influence on Halloween Town. To create an etched effect, the crew painted all of the buildings black and then brushed white accents on top to make them look like a drawing. Although most of the palette is monochrome, there are hints of orange and green throughout the town. "The orange came from streetlights made of pumpkins and the Halloween-inspired designs," Taylor explains. "For the green,

Halloween Town has a muted color palette and a Gothic visual style.

SCHEMING SONG
LOCK SHOCK BARREL

KA

The filmmakers sketched multiple
versions of Halloween Town before
building the massive set.

DT

Above: The Halloween Town set with The Mayor's car;
Right: Inhabitants of Halloween Town.

the backstory was that there is a toxic green, poisonous underground river. So wherever there's a drain or a manhole cover that's off, the green light will shine up through it. That gave us the chance to either warm up a shot or cool it down, but still stay within the range of black, white, and orange."

The Halloween Town set was a massive construction, created in a circular structure, and it was also a massive challenge to figure out. Pieces had to move so the animators and camera operators could enter the set. It featured buildings surrounding the town square, as well as the graveyard and city hall. It was the most difficult part of the world to actually build, but underscores the handmade quality of the film.

"We had a bird's-eye view plan of it and a model that was sliced up like a pie," Lookinland says. "Then it was up to us to recreate that four times bigger. All of the shapes were so out of control and so wacky that there's no standard building practice. There was a lot of problem solving to do. But part of what I think resonates with this film is that it really does have this handmade quality look to it, and that shows on the screen. I think you feel it somehow when you watch it."

Jack's House

Jack's house, located in Halloween Town, defies the known laws of physics. Art director Deane Taylor inverted the towering structure, which sits atop a hill, purposefully making it "upside down and sort of strange." It has an eyeball doorknob and a spider doorbell pull, which screams to announce visitors. Its gaunt lines and unusual design evoke Jack himself, and the designers weren't concerned with realism in its design. "The way we were building it we could make these fanciful things that wouldn't work in the real world," explained Lookinland. "That stuff was a lot of fun to build."

Sally feels trapped by the confines of her bedroom in the Evil Scientist's lab.

Evil Scientist's Lab

The Evil Scientist builds his creations in a laboratory, which has the appearance of a water tower but it actually echoes the design of the doctor's head. Inside is Sally's bedroom, which has an elevated window from which she eventually escapes, and the kitchen where she prepares his meals.

"The shape of the Evil Scientist's head is the shape of his laboratory, which is like a cartoon of his big head," says Heinrichs. "Everything has a certain meaning and a connection to the character that it's associated with—The Mayor to his car, Jack to his house, Sally and her room and how she escapes the room, and the environs of Halloween Town. All those things are, as they always are in animation, very character-based."

The creation of Oogie Boogie's lair.

Oogie Boogie's Lair

Oogie Boogie's cavernous lair was the
most challenging set to conceive and build.
Taylor describes the set piece as a dungeon
with casino décor, and it took several
months of sketching to land on the final
design. Selick came up with the idea to use
UV paint and UV lights, which gave the
scenes an off-kilter vibe that feels fitting
for the larger-than-life villain. The lair
looks one way with the lights off, revealing
torture devices and jagged steel, and another
with the lights illuminated. To achieve that,
the art department looked to both casinos and
cave drawings for inspiration. One particular
torture device was a roulette wheel, which had
to actually work.

"The spinning casino wheel lights up and
it's got hearts and clubs and diamonds and
spades, as well as skeleton heads," Lookinland
remembers. "That set was so fun to build
because it had this whole mechanical aspect to
spin. It had a super simple motor with a bicycle
chain, but it was difficult to build that."

The Hinterlands

Jack discovers seven magical trees located in the Hinterlands, a mysterious in-between land that acts as a gateway to and from Halloween Town. Each tree opens a doorway to a different holiday-themed world: Christmas, Halloween, Valentine's Day, Easter, St. Patrick's Day, Independence Day, and Thanksgiving. Jack, of course, selects the Christmas doorway, with the image of a decorated Christmas tree. Burton drew the grove when he was conceptualizing the film and transforming the trees into a viable set was a major challenge.

"I think they stood about three meters tall," Taylor remembers. "They had to be big enough for Jack, who was quite tall, to fall into comfortably. There was one shot where he opens the doorknob on the Christmas Town tree, so the scale started from the doorknob and his hand."

Jack discovers a door to a new holiday world.

Christmas Town

Christmas Town was the first set that was built for the film, and the filmmakers embraced a more whimsical, warm look for the home of Sandy Claws. Set designer Gregg Olsen described the set as "Dr. Seuss meets Dr. Caligari" while Taylor notes that the inspiration was a European postcard created by Dr. Seuss. Notably, Christmas Town features the film's only illuminated night sky. "Jack's first view of Christmas Town includes the only stars in the movie," said Kozachik. "We built a dozen or two: a black card with cutout pointy stars taped to clamp lights. Pressed from behind a blue muslin backing was a night sky with movable stars."

Assistant art director Kendal Cronkhite was responsible for the design of Christmas Town and wanted it to be "soft and sloppy." With its rolling lines and vibrant lights, the set also needed to act as an apt juxtaposition with Jack's hometown. "It's Dr. Seuss and bright colors, like candy," she explained. "And then there's Halloween Town, which is German Expressionist, odd angles, on-edge, off-kilter."

Whimsical concept art for Christmas Town.

Spiral Hill

At the beginning of the film, Jack Skellington walks along Spiral Hill, overlooking the cemetery, where he and Sally later reunite at the end. The moonlit hill, which appeared in Burton's original sketches, was not just another set, but in fact was a puppet itself. "As Jack walks down the uncurling branch, it looks too spindly to hold Jack's weight," explained Kozachik. "We didn't use invisible wire or any post-opticals. Tim Hittle preferred to animate with a beefy armature inside the branch, just like another puppet, attached to Jack's feet." The hill purposefully is less jagged and angular than the rest of the sets, evoking a Christmas card covered in glitter and hinting at a romantic atmosphere.

The construction of Spiral Hill.

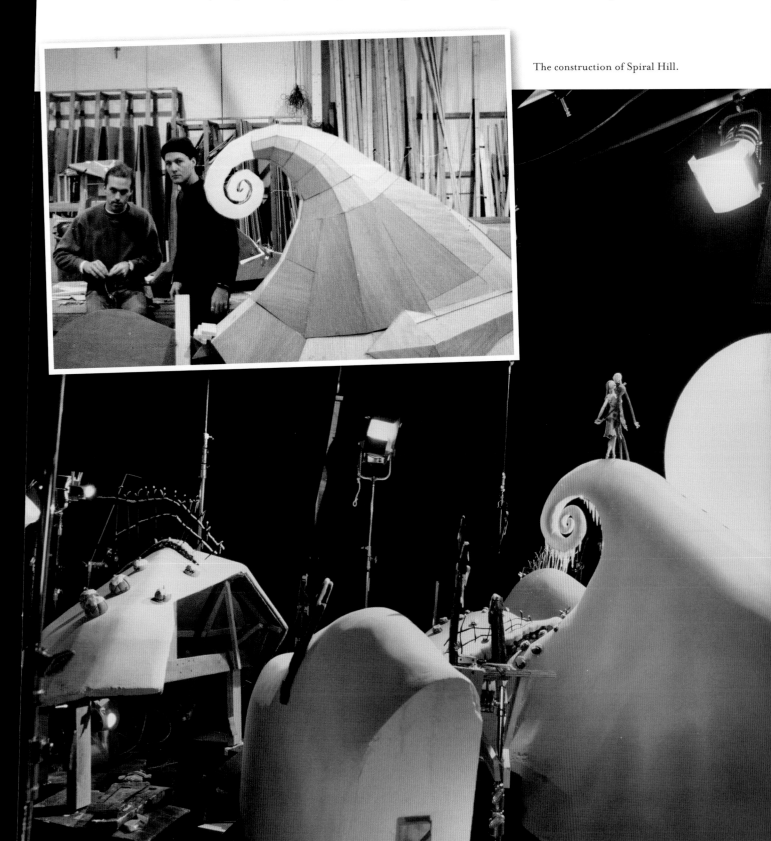

The Real World

When Jack takes over Christmas and boards his sleigh to deliver gifts to children, he has to venture out in the real world—a place that exists separately from the holiday lands. It's purposefully straight, designed in an isometric pattern, to ensure it would stand out from the more fantastical aesthetics of Halloween Town and Christmas Town. "We wanted to make it look like the least interesting part of the world," Taylor says. "We ended up with this very awkward and difficult task, especially things like building staircases isometrically. But we were able to create a distorted reality that became as justified as the other two worlds."

Below: Houses for the Real World. *Right:* A sketch of Jack as Santa Claus.

The Holidays

Tim Burton's The Nightmare Before Christmas was initially released to coincide with Halloween in the fall of 1993; however, the film and its story clearly also embrace Christmas. Fans have long debated which holiday the movie belongs to, but both Halloween and Christmas play into the lore—and allure—of the film. Three of Burton's films, *Edward Scissorhands* (1990), *Batman Returns* (1992), and *Tim Burton's The Nightmare Before Christmas*, which were made in succession, are set at Christmastime.

"I've exorcised my Christmas demons," Burton reflected after making *Nightmare*. "Growing up in Burbank, I responded to the holidays, especially Halloween and Christmas, because they were the most visual and fun in some respects. The best I can decipher from the whole thing is that when you grow up in a blank environment, any form of ritual, like a holiday, gives you a sense of place."

A still from Burton's film *Batman Returns*, also set during the Christmas season.

THE FINAL FILM

On February 21, 1993, *Tim Burton's The Nightmare Before Christmas* wrapped production. There were still a few lingering special effects that needed to be completed, but because stop-motion animation relies on what is captured on camera the film was already largely complete. Everyone had a sense that what they had done was innovative, unique, and compelling, particularly as it embraced Burton's initial vision even after two years of development and evolution. It was a singular experience for the filmmakers.

"It was so much fun, like an adventure every day," the film's artistic coordinator Allison Abbate reflects. "When you're shooting on film, you never know if the shot came through until you see it projected. So you'd be sitting in dailies at seven o'clock in the morning and just biting your nails hoping that a light didn't turn off or something didn't fall unnoticed in the background of the shot. That kind of stress bonds you with the team. It's like being in a war together. When it works, it is an amazing feeling, and I think we've all been chasing that high for the rest of our lives."

"It was just a remarkable group of people," adds animator Trey Thomas. "I've worked on a bunch of movies and that group was the most symbiotic. Everybody had each other's back, working toward one goal. It's never happened since. I've been on a lot of great, fun movies, but there was a cohesiveness on that one that you can't design—it just happens. I think we all look back on it as one of the big highlights, if not the highlight, of our careers."

Sally and friends applaud Jack's entrance in the movie's opening number, "This is Halloween."

Though Jack and the other residents of Halloween Town try their best to throw a winning Christmas, they eventually learn the importance of embracing their strengths.

2

WELCOME BACK

CONTINUING THE CELEBRATION

When *Tim Burton's The Nightmare Before Christmas* first arrived in theaters in 1993, audiences were unsure what to make of it. Was it a Halloween movie or a Christmas movie? Was it for kids or adults? Was it a musical or a horror film? The film didn't look or sound like recent Walt Disney Studios animated features, such as *The Little Mermaid* (1989). It was being released via Touchstone Pictures, a distributor that typically unleashed more mature fare. It was also an outlier alongside other contemporary popular movies: Beloved family flicks in 1993 included more conventional stories like *The Sandlot* and *The Secret Garden*. This, the story of a misfit skeleton seeking his place in a fantastical world, was less easily defined, making it more challenging to sell to audiences.

"They thought the movie was very dark and would scare little kids," producer Denise Di Novi recalls about Disney's decision to release the film as part of Touchstone Pictures. "It is darker than the average animated movie. It's hard to believe now, but when we made *Batman Returns*, people thought, 'Oh my, it's so dark and disturbing.' If you watch it now it's so tame compared to the *Batman* movies that came after. It shows you how times have changed. But Disney thought *Nightmare* was too scary for little kids."

Still, *Tim Burton's The Nightmare Before Christmas* earned a modest $51 million at the box office and garnered positive reviews from critics. Roger Ebert praised the film's innovation and uniqueness, writing, "One of the many pleasures of *Tim Burton's The Nightmare Before Christmas* is that there is not a single recognizable landscape within it. Everything looks strange and haunting. Even Santa Claus would be difficult to recognize without his red-and-white uniform." Peter Travers added in *Rolling Stone* that the film "has the earmarks of an enduring classic. Of all the new Halloween films, only this one has the power to truly haunt our dreams."

The feature premiered at the New York Film Festival on October 9, 1993, and then had its Hollywood premiere on October 14, 1993, at the El Capitan Theatre in Los Angeles, which was attended by several members of the cast and crew. There was also a star-studded event on Halloween for the release of the picture book *The Nightmare Before Christmas*, attended by Burton, Catherine O'Hara, and even Phil Collins, who brought along a young Lily Collins, dressed as a princess. Despite some modest promotion, including bus stop ads and a Burger King campaign, the response to the film was relatively tepid.

"It was highly regarded for its visual audacity and for the lively story," Chris Sarandon says. "But I don't recall there being this big groundswell,

Top: The film's theatrical poster; *Bottom:* A flyer for the New York Film Festival.

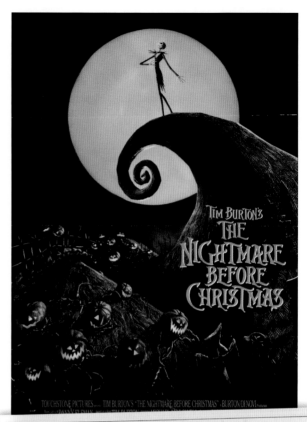

New York Film Festival
Alice Tully Hall: Saturday, October 9, 1993, at 9:00 p.m.
Sunday, October 10, 1993, at 1:30 p.m.

TIM BURTON'S
THE NIGHTMARE BEFORE CHRISTMAS
USA, 1993

Director: Henry Selick
Producers: Tim Burton and Denise Di Novi
Co-Producer: Kathleen Gavin
Production Company: Touchstone Pictures
Photography: Pete Kozachik
Editor: Stan Webb
Music: Danny Elfman
Art Director: Deane Taylor
Visual Consultant: Rick Heinrichs
Animation Supervisor: Eric Leighton
Character Supervisor: John Reed
Storyboard Supervisor: Joe Ranft
Puppet Fabrication: Bonita De Carlo
Set Construction: Bo Henry
Set and Model Supervisor: Mitch Romanauski
Production Manager: Phil Lofaro
Running time: 75 minutes
A Touchstone Pictures Release
World Premiere

Voices:
Jack Skellington: Chris Sarandon and Danny Elfman
Sally: Catherine O'Hara
The Mayor: Glenn Shadix
Oogie Boogie: Ken Page
Lock: Paul Reubens
Shock: Catherine O'Hara
Barrel: Danny Elfman
The Evil Scientist: William Hickey

Tim Burton's fascination with parades and public holidays colliding with dark forces here finds its full flowering when the people of Halloweentown decide to take over Christmas. The innovative stop-motion animation is like a pop-up book run amuck. Cheer for tender Jack the pumpkin king, recoil from Oogie Boogie, a mysterious menace who looks like and just might be a day-glow green sock, weep for Sally the rag doll whose special trick is coming apart at the seams. As fiction illuminates the darker truth of fact, this musical fantasy exposes the darker truth of the joy of giving.

Short: VINCENT / USA / 1982
Director: Tim Burton / *Running time:* 9 minutes
A delightful puppet animation about a boy who wishes he had some scary secrets.

32C

TIM BURTON'S
NIGHTMARE BEFORE CHRISTMAS

October 6, 1993

Dear Friend,

Enclosed is your ticket for the special party following the
screening of Tim Burton's NIGHTMARE BEFORE CHRISTMAS.   The
party will take place on a special tented area on the
grounds of Lincoln Center.

The screening, which begins at 9:15 p.m., will be held at:

THE BRUNO WALTER AUDITORIUM
The New York Library for The Performing Arts
40 Lincoln Center Plaza
(111 Amsterdam at 65th Street)

If you find you cannot attend, or have any questions, please
call me or ▮▮▮▮▮▮▮▮▮▮▮ in my office at ▮▮▮▮▮▮▮▮.

All the best,

Diana Loomis

Diana Loomis
Director
East Coast Publicity

An invitation to the film's New York Film Festival
party; *Inset (left):* Tim Burton at the film's premiere;
Inset (right): French press for the film.

a *Star Wars* kind of response to a movie. It was muted. It didn't blow up. But it's certainly blown up over time."

For the filmmakers, there was a sense of disappointment as the movie came and went. The crew had spent two years meticulously crafting the world of Halloween Town and its inhabitants, and once it disappeared from theaters there was a sense that Jack Skellington and pals had vanished from the cultural zeitgeist. While the film had built a small fan base and some merchandise, including a Bone Daddy T-shirt, could be found in stores, *Tim Burton's The Nightmare Before Christmas* initially appeared to have been a fleeting creation.

"It came and went pretty quickly and didn't do very well," Elfman reflected around the film's twenty-fifth anniversary. "Nobody understood what it was or how to market it. I put so much into this project, including so much of my own personality, that it really hurt. At the time I was really depressed after it came out. I put so much into it and it was gone."

Selick and Burton understood the initial reluctance of audiences to fill the theaters. *Tim Burton's The Nightmare Before Christmas* was an unusual movie, about unusual characters singing unusual songs. But both filmmakers were certain the artistry and the vision were there. Despite the public's reaction, *Nightmare* had a soul that very few movies possess, and there was something about it that felt more important than simple box office numbers.

"It made its money and then quietly seemed to go away," Selick recalls. "And so it was bittersweet. We absolutely never expected it to be a huge blockbuster, like the other Disney films that came before and after. None of the films I've worked on have been blockbusters, but when they're good, they last. And then they start to grow."

"I never forgot about it because it's one of those projects that was deep inside me," Burton adds. "Even if it was a complete bomb I wouldn't have forgotten about it."

Tim Burton signs copies of *The Nightmare Before Christmas*.

A year after the film's release in theaters, on September 30, 1994, Touchstone Home Video released *Tim Burton's The Nightmare Before Christmas* on VHS. The DVD followed on December 2, 1997. It was during those early years that the film's fan base began to slowly flourish. The movie was shared by families and friends in their living rooms, and many viewers adopted it as an annual tradition to watch every Halloween or every Christmas—or both. As more and more people discovered it, more and more people began watching it each year. "It got a cult following right away because Tim has a very loyal following," Di Novi notes. "His following loved it. But it took a few years until it became a perennial Halloween movie."

A GROWING AUDIENCE

There were a lot of factors that played into the gradual growth of the film's fan base, but for many the central reason is the film's original artistic vision. "There was a really simple thing: It is just really good," film historian Ian Nathan explains. "It's really charming and visually wonderful, so it just carries you along. And great films find their audience. That started to happen with *The Nightmare Before Christmas*. People bought it on DVD and they started to watch it repeatedly."

Burton himself isn't completely sure what's been behind the ever-expanding phenomenon of the film. Like the making of the movie, attempting to understand its success has been like trying to capture lightning in a bottle. It's a once-in-a-lifetime occurrence that has ultimately been generated by the fans themselves.

Jack Skellington welcomes fans to the El Capitan Theatre; *Inset:* A poster for the re-release of the film in Disney Digital 3D.

Left (top and bottom): Burton and the voice cast gathered for the 3D re-release of the film in 2006; *Right:* Tim Burton and Helena Bonham Carter at the film's re-release premiere in Venice in 2006.

"I think it just had enough of a core thing and they re-released it and it gained traction," Burton says. "There are certain things that historically have happened that way and it's hard to predict why, like *The Rocky Horror Picture Show*. I would look at it as, something to achieve is a holiday kind of thing that is sort of a perennial."

In 2000, Touchstone Home Video re-released *Tim Burton's The Nightmare Before Christmas* as a special edition DVD with bonus features, including audio commentary from Selick, a making-of feature, and deleted scenes. By the mid-2000s, Walt Disney Pictures, recognizing the immense fan base and the opportunities to grow the property, brought the film back under their official umbrella. The studio converted *Nightmare* to Disney Digital 3D and, on October 20, 2006, re-released the film in theaters, with special presentations at the Venice Film Festival and the London Film Festival. For

Burton, the 3D re-release emphasized the hallmark magic of stop-motion film.

"I love things in 3D," he explains. "It took me back to when you're on the set looking at these puppets and the tactile nature of the sets. The 3D actually brought you more into what that world was like. In this particular case, I felt like it enhanced what the artists did—you could feel the texture of the puppets and I thought it was great. I loved it. You can't say that about everything, but for this it brought you closer to being on a set and feeling these characters. I was very happy with the outcome of that."

That stop-motion format is also part of the enduring legacy of the movie. There's a tangible, handmade quality to the film, almost as though the viewer could reach out and touch the characters and their world. It allows the story to feel even more immersive and immediate,

Novels and Books

For many years, *Tim Burton's The Nightmare Before Christmas* was a stand-alone story. While the characters lived on in fan fiction and fan art, as well as games and merchandise, only recently has the tale of Jack Skellington and his friends continued in other forms. While Burton has been approached to make a sequel to *Nightmare*, the filmmaker has always rejected the idea—especially in any form other than traditional stop-motion. Burton is, however, open to expanding the world of Halloween Town through games or novels when it makes sense, particularly if it allows a character or aspect of the story to be illuminated from a fresh perspective.

"I resisted doing sequels because it is what it is," Burton explains. "I want the film to exist rather than go, 'Let's have Jack go to Thanksgiving world or torment the Easter Bunny more or whatever.' There's a purity to it and it goes back to the stop-motion, but the books and toys look at it in a different way. I didn't want to do a film like that because I felt it would take away from the purity of what the original is."

In 2020, Disney Manga released *Tim Burton's The Nightmare Before Christmas: Zero's Journey*, written by D.J. Milky and illustrated by Kei Ishiyama, David Hutchison, Dan Conner, and Kiyoshi Arai. In the comic book, Zero goes missing from Halloween Town and is forced to find his way home via Christmas Town, offering a deeper look at Jack's trusty companion. Many of the film's characters, including The Mayor, Sally, and Lock, Shock, and Barrel, returned for the comic. Another manga series, *Tim Burton's The Nightmare Before Christmas: Mirror Moon*, ran for five issues from 2021 until 2022. Written by Mallory Reaves with artwork by Gabriella Chianello and Nataliya Torretta, the series centered on Sally as she took over Halloween planning for Jack. This one also featured familiar characters from the film, such as the beloved vampire brothers.

The most significant expansion of *Tim Burton's The Nightmare Before Christmas* arrived in 2022 with *Long Live the Pumpkin Queen*, a young adult novel by writer Shea Ernshaw. The book follows the events of *Nightmare*, shifting the perspective to Sally, who has recently married Jack, and detailing her adventures in the newly-discovered Dream Town.

"The whole story came to me all at once," Ernshaw says. "I had this notion of Sally and Jack, and wanting to see what happens with their relationship. In the movie, we get to see Jack and the nightmare that he creates on Christmas Eve. I thought, 'Well, the juxtaposition of nightmares is dreams.' I knew it needed to be a story about dreams, so naturally, the Sandman was going to be the villain. I also wanted to explore more of Sally's background and her origin."

Although Sally is an essential character in the film, viewers learn more about Jack than they do about the practical and persistent rag doll, who was originally crafted by screenwriter Caroline Thompson. In the novel, Sally's history and her true parents are revealed, as well as her own hopes and dreams for the future. For Ernshaw, *Long Live the Pumpkin Queen* is a way for Sally to finally be the protagonist after all these years.

"I kept coming back to who Sally was and the stories I think she would have wanted to tell," Ernshaw says. "I really tried to be true to her. That was a question I asked myself as I was writing: Is this really Sally? Is this what Sally would want? She's waited a really long time to have the story told, so I wanted to do it justice and give her the story she deserved."

The book cover for Shea Ernshaw's continuation of Sally's story.

which helps it to stand out amid the computer-generated (CG) animation that has taken over Hollywood since its release.

"There is something to the idea that this thing actually exists," Selick says. "Its flaws are in the animation and the imperfections are like a clue that it's real. You'd never have those with CG. You inherently know this exists and it was touched by humans."

Alongside its handmade artistry, the film showcases Burton's particular style. It's unusual for an animated work in Hollywood to reflect an individual vision, rather than that of a studio itself. The convergence of the filmmaker's singular style with the careful skill of Selick and the crew's stop-motion prowess resulted in something completely stand-alone.

"Certainly people respond to hand-drawn films and digitally-created films with a lot of passion," associate producer Phil Lofaro notes. "But this is a film that is uniquely Tim Burton. And you can't look at that film and not see his hand. None of the other animated films are really like that. Even with the hand-drawn stuff from Disney nothing looks like one person's vision the way that *Nightmare* does."

"I don't want to be hyperbolic, but I think it's a masterpiece," Di Novi adds. "Who else besides Tim would interweave Halloween and Christmas like that? At the core, the emotionality of the character being so different and yearning to be accepted—which is in all of Tim's work—is always going to be meaningful to people. I think it's one of the greatest animated movies in history."

The constant re-releases, which have continued over the years in various forms, including a 4D version that incorporated additional elements like fog and snow into the viewing experience, have played into the growth of *Tim Burton's The Nightmare Before Christmas*. But the movie's popularity is also connected to that message of learning to belong. Although *Nightmare* was of its time when it was made, the story and its themes transcend a specific era or trend. Burton has always incorporated universal ideas into his films, but the director's

fascination with an outcast finding acceptance felt especially poignant in a family-friendly, holiday film. Many film historians and critics have pointed to that universality as one of the reasons *Nightmare* has continued to captivate audiences for generations. Viewers young and old, from all backgrounds and walks of life, can connect with Jack's search for meaning and eventual understanding that everything he's ever wanted has been in front of him all along.

"The continuing popularity of this movie probably has something to do with its message," author Edwin Page wrote in *Gothic Fantasy: The Films of Tim Burton*. "It is about staying true to yourself, despite failures, despite misunderstanding. Through Jack's failure to bring seasonal goodwill the film also tells us that not everything in life will work out the way we want it to. This is an important message, especially for children who are often force fed 'happily ever after' endings that give them a false perspective on life. *The Nightmare Before Christmas* presents something more real, though woven into a fantastical narrative."

Jack's story resonated with the filmmakers and the crew as much it resonates with fans. The emotional core of the film, along with the impressive artistry and tactile nature of the stop-motion craft, have allowed the movie to transcend generations. Against all odds, *Tim Burton's The Nightmare Before Christmas* has become the exact thing that inspired it in the first place—a perennial holiday favorite.

"I would always get very excited as a child to watch those holiday films that created the sense of an event to me," Burton says. "It was an event that you look forward to on television. I wanted to create something that gave me the kinds of feelings I had when I was growing up watching those classics. I was always very proud of *Nightmare* and loved it, but at the time when it came out it wasn't what it's turned into. It's been a journey to get there. It makes me happy because it took a long time for that to happen, but it was always something that I felt satisfied that instinct for me."

The film's presence at San Diego Comic Con has helped expand its reach.

Continuing the Stop-Motion Tradition

Although stop-motion animation existed long before *Tim Burton's The Nightmare Before Christmas*, the filmmakers used innovative techniques that helped pave the way for films to come. Many of the crew went on to work on future stop-motion animated features and Burton himself has made several more, including a full-length adaptation of his 1984 live-action short *Frankenweenie*. *Nightmare*'s legacy goes far beyond its world and characters, and, in fact, the film helped to open audiences' minds to the visual possibilities of cinema and storytelling.

"It felt special at the time and unique at the time because of the stop-motion," Burton reflects. "There have been more than usual stop-motion features since, including *Corpse Bride* and *Frankenweenie*. I've always wanted to keep a hand in it because it's a medium that I love."

James and the Giant Peach (1996)

Following *Tim Burton's The Nightmare Before Christmas*, director Henry Selick went on to helm *James and the Giant Peach*, a feature adaptation of Roald Dahl's 1961 children's novel. The film, a combination of stop-motion animation and live action, was produced by Burton and Denise Di Novi. The stop-motion scenes were filmed in Skellington studio, with many of the same crew members as *Nightmare*, and Jack himself even popped up in the movie in a cameo as one of the pirates. Joe Ranft, who worked on the storyboards for *Nightmare*, suggested the idea for the movie, although it never achieved the kind of legacy *Nightmare* now has. "We had an incredible crew and the animation is beautiful," Selick says of the film. "The look is beautiful."

Tim Burton's Corpse Bride (2005)

Burton joined forces with Mike Johnson to direct *Tim Burton's Corpse Bride*, a stop-motion fantasy set in Victorian England. Like *Nightmare*, *Corpse Bride* centered on a misfit protagonist, Victor Van Dort, who falls in love with an unlikely heroine. Many of *Nightmare*'s crew returned, including cinematographer Pete Kozachik, for the production, which took place in London. Elfman also teamed up with Burton again to write the score, as well as

four musical numbers performed by the voice cast. The filmmaker was able to draw a direct link to his female lead from *Nightmare* while creating *Corpse Bride*, which was based on an old fable he was introduced to, again, by Ranft. "One of the things I enjoyed in *Nightmare* was the emotional quality that the Sally character had: there was something there that I liked," Burton said. "It's nice to get emotion in animation. And also I was thinking about expanding my female characters. So thinking about *Corpse Bride* was trying to do something with that emotional quality to it."

Coraline (2009)

Coraline, directed by Selick and based on Neil Gaiman's novella of the same name, marked the first feature-length film by the emerging animation studio Laika. In a similar vein to *Tim Burton's The Nightmare Before Christmas*, the movie centered on a protagonist who discovers a secret door into another world. Upon its release, *Coraline* became the third-highest-grossing stop-motion film of all time and was nominated for the Oscar for Best Animated Feature. "We shot it in 3D and actually beat the film *Avatar* for Best 3D Film of the year by the International 3D Society," Selick remembers. "It was really a great experience. Everything we did was built on what we already learned on the previous films."

Frankenweenie (2012)

One of Burton's earliest films was the live-action short *Frankenweenie*, an homage to *Frankenstein*. In 2012, Burton revisited the story, remaking it as a 3D stop-motion animated feature for Walt Disney Pictures. The comedy-horror movie, with music by Elfman, became the first stop-motion film to be released in IMAX 3D, and was nominated for an Oscar, a Golden Globe, and a BAFTA. The tale of a reanimated family dog has a dark-yet-emotional tone similar to *Nightmare*, as well as the same tangible quality. "It's great that you can pick up the puppets and touch them," Burton said of the film. "It's like an old movie, doing your water reflections with mirrors, doing one frame at a time. I liked the idea of going back to that, it does reenergize the spirit."

Wendell & Wild (2022)

Selick's most recent foray into stop-motion animation, Netflix feature *Wendell & Wild*, arrived in 2022. Written with Jordan Peele, the film was based on an unpublished book by Selick and Clay McLeod Chapman. Peele and Keegan-Michael Key voiced the lead characters in an original story following two demon brothers who escape from the underworld. A few of the animators from *Nightmare*, including Anthony Scott, worked on the film with Selick—yet another example of *Nightmare*'s enduring legacy.

A YEAR-ROUND HOLIDAY

The debate as to whether *Tim Burton's The Nightmare Before Christmas* is a Halloween movie or a Christmas movie rages on decades later. Many people embrace the film as an annual tradition around both holidays, but there's no denying its strong connection with Halloween. Growing up in Burbank, Burton was obsessed with both holidays, often decorating his Christmas tree with Halloween-inspired ornaments. To the filmmakers, there's a similar spirit that connects both events.

"Halloween was my favorite and it always seemed to be the festive season from Halloween to Christmas," Burton remembers. "So it's an extended holiday to me, so to speak, and in my house Christmas and Halloween got jumbled up. I kept Halloween going. I always enjoyed the light of Christmas, but Halloween was a bit darker, and that's where the juxtaposition of things in the film came from."

Prior to the release of *Tim Burton's The Nightmare Before Christmas*, there were a few Halloween films beloved by moviegoing audiences. *The Rocky Horror Picture Show* had come out in 1975 and transformed into a cult classic, but it was largely for a mature audience. *Nightmare* offered something new for those who loved eerie things with a less terrifying feel, as did its contemporary *Hocus Pocus*, released the same year.

"I think *Nightmare* helped to restore some of Halloween's whimsical quality, especially in regards to its cinematic portrayals," explains author Lisa Morton. "Halloween is a festival that has been impacted by film before—John Carpenter's 1978 classic *Halloween* helped steer Halloween celebrations more towards adults—but *Nightmare* appealed to many fans of the holiday by emphasizing playfulness, joy, and creativity."

The popularity of the film as a holiday tradition was aided by the fact that there was nothing else like it for either Halloween or Christmas. "It's not

Many fans decorate their homes for Halloween with characters from the film.

Top: A Jack Skellington Christmas stocking; *Left:* Jack welcomes visitors during the holiday season; *Right:* An inflatable Jack and Zero.

Celebrity Tributes and Halloween Costumes

Jack, Sally, and the Halloween Town crew have cemented themselves in pop culture in numerous ways, but none so obvious as the elaborate Halloween costumes worn by the film's most famous fans. Since the release of *Tim Burton's The Nightmare Before Christmas*, everyone from Gwen Stefani to Channing Tatum to Joey King have dressed as the characters to celebrate Halloween. Many of the costumes have been custom creations, with makeup, wigs, and masks to match, and each one has had a unique flair. One of the most memorable interpretations

Left: Michelle Trachtenberg; *Right*: Joey King.

was in 2011, when actress Michelle Trachtenberg reimagined Sally for Heidi Klum's annual Halloween party. Melissa Joan Hart, Nicole Richie, Vanessa Hudgens, and Austin Butler have all joined the fun over the years.

While most of the notable costumes have been worn as part of Halloween, some celebrities have brought the world of *Nightmare* to other celebrations throughout the years as well. Khloé Kardashian and Kendall Jenner dressed as Sally and Jack for their nephew Mason Disick's fourth birthday, which was themed around the film, in 2014, while Ariana Grande donned a Jack Skellington-inspired ensemble onstage in 2015. Rita Ora also wore a *Nightmare* homage at the 2013 Parklife Festival in Manchester, England. It's clear that love for Burton's creation extends far and wide.

Below: Ariana Grande; *Right:* Rita Ora.

a traditional Christmas film or holiday film," says
Brian Volk-Weiss, director of *The Holiday Movies
That Made Us*. "It can be a scary movie, depending
on your age. But there are a lot of incredibly
sophisticated, complicated characters and
personalities. The plot itself is extremely simple, but
the characters in the plot are so complicated."

The intersection of Halloween and Christmas
in *Tim Burton's The Nightmare Before Christmas* is
obvious. But since its release, the film has evolved
into a classic viewing for Valentine's Day, Easter,
Thanksgiving, and more recent semi-holidays like
Halfway to Halloween and Halfway to Christmas.
These holidays fit in with the original story, too: Jack
is the Pumpkin King of Halloween Town and involves
himself in the holiday of Christmas, but numerous
holiday doorways exist in the Hinterlands and the
Easter Bunny has a small, but essential, role in the
film. Although *Nightmare* may have initially cemented
itself as a specific annual tradition, over the past
decade it has also become a 365-day celebration.

This expansion has been aided by several
factors, including extensive and constant
merchandising and the film's frequent presence
at various fan conventions, including San Diego
Comic Con, which takes place yearly in July.
"Comic Con was a huge gateway for fans," notes
Elise Barkan, Director of Franchise Development
and Activation at Disney Parks, Experiences and
Products. "Once we saw the success at Comic
Con, we showed up with *The Nightmare Before
Christmas* in a whole host of ways."

Tim Burton's The Nightmare Before Christmas
has trickled into celebrations for Valentine's
Day thanks to Jack and Sally's memorable love
story. Hallmark sells *Nightmare*-themed cards for
couples. Many fans host Thanksgiving dinners
inspired by the world of the film, a fact that is less
surprising than one might initially assume. Several
writers and film critics, in fact, have argued that
Nightmare is actually a Thanksgiving movie.

"Jack Skellington's harrowing journey from
Pumpkin King to disgraced Santa imposter
seriously lends itself to Thanksgiving's themes of
gratefulness and family," Alison Foreman wrote
for *Mashable* in 2021. "It's a narrative genuinely

suited to what this holiday is supposed to be about, even if it's totally devoid of gourds and cranberry sauce… What makes me confident *The Nightmare Before Christmas* is a Thanksgiving movie are those themes of thankfulness. Ultimately, they're what this animated classic is really about. It wasn't the set dressing that helped Jack save Christmas. And all the jack-o-lanterns and boughs of holly in the world can't overcome the soul-affirming experience of real gratitude."

For many, it makes complete sense that *Tim Burton's The Nightmare Before Christmas* has found a year-round audience. "The film resonates with so many people, so they make it their own," explains George McClements, Director of Concept Art and Story Development at Disney Parks, Experiences and Products. "The fact that we see the turkey door means that Jack can go to Thanksgiving Town. The fact that we see the four-leaf clover means he can go to St. Patrick's Day Town. And obviously Jack is going to go. He's not going to say 'I'm done' after he visits Christmas Town. He's not that character. So that's why we celebrate all year."

Perhaps the most meaningful aspect of a holiday like Thanksgiving or Christmas is the gathering of friends and family around a common table to enjoy a communal meal. Even for Halloween, with its tradition of trick-or-treating, food is a focal point—usually in the form of candy or sweets. Because these celebrations are so closely linked with cooking and dining, *Nightmare* often inspires the holiday meal itself. In fact, several cookbooks have been released for the fans of the film, encouraging home chefs to incorporate the aesthetic and themes of the movie into their holiday spreads.

The Nightmare Before Dinner: Recipes to Die For: The Beetle House Cookbook, released in 2018, was compiled by Zach Neil, chef of Beetle House, a Halloween-inspired restaurant based in New York City and Los Angeles. The unauthorized cookbook includes recipes and cocktail ideas intended for fans of Tim Burton and Halloween, including dishes like Frog's Breath and Nightshade Risotto. *The Nightmare Before Christmas: The Official Cookbook & Entertaining Guide*, released in 2021, features recipes and party-planning ideas for fans. It's not for the faint of heart, though: Dishes include Dr. Finkelstein Bite-Sized "Brain" Puff Pies and Oogie Boogie Pasta Worms.

Themed cookbooks encourage fans to create their own *Nightmare* dishes.

IN THE PARKS

It was only a matter of time before Jack and Sally would visit the Disney Parks. On October 5, 2001, *Haunted Mansion Holiday* arrived at Disneyland. The annual overlay, which takes over the iconic attraction each fall from Halloween through January without impacting the original attraction's structure, was conceived in the late 1990s.

"It was very clear that this audience were huge fans of *The Nightmare Before Christmas*, but perhaps there wasn't enough momentum for a standalone *Nightmare Before Christmas* attraction," explains Todd Martens, a Los Angeles-based journalist who has written extensively about Disneyland and the Disney Parks in general. "But there was enough momentum to redo *Haunted Mansion* for the holidays. At Disneyland this is something that happens with more regularity than at Walt Disney World, in part because Disneyland is a locals park. It was Disney recognizing that *The Nightmare Before Christmas* had become an important cult film and that its audience was gravitating toward Disneyland and the *Haunted Mansion*."

The concept also came about after the Imagineers asked themselves what sort of holiday celebration might occur in the beloved attraction. "We were walking by *Haunted Mansion* one day and we were like, 'Oh, what if Santa landed on that house? What might it be?'" explained Walt Disney Imagineering's Steve Davison. "And that's really how it all was born." He added, "Artistically it was a big challenge because you have two opposing forces: You have the *Haunted Mansion*, which has a very classic design, and then you have the *Nightmare* style."

The intention wasn't necessarily to recreate the film as a Disney Parks attraction. Instead, the Imagineers wanted to draw on beloved elements of the movie, including the Christmas countdown clock, Jack's sleigh, the vampire teddy bear, and Zero, and bring them into the *Haunted Mansion* in an organic way. The film inspired much of the design, which feels like a logical extension of Halloween Town. "The colors were all predetermined for us, because when you look at the film it's all orange, purple, black, red," noted illustrator Tim Wollweber, who created many

The *Haunted Mansion Holiday* at Disneyland.

Above: The Oogie Boogie Bash; *Inset:* A set piece from the
Haunted Mansion Holiday.

of the visual elements in the overlay. "It was just
putting that all together to make these wacky
patterns and pointy skulls."

A focal point of the attraction's overlay is
Spiral Hill, which is covered in snow and dozens
of glowing pumpkin heads. The mountain, which
dangles with icicles, towers over guests inside
the attraction. It's another example of how the
Imagineers took the film and made it their own.
"The concept for the snow mountain, of course,
came from the film," explained Brian Sandahl,
former art director of *Haunted Mansion Holiday*,
adding, "We're not trying to recreate the movie.
We're inspired by the movie, so we're taking that big
piece that is very familiar to people that know the film
inside and out and we stuck that in the graveyard."

Many of the film's actors, notably Chris
Sarandon, Ken Page, and Catherine O'Hara,
reprised their character voices for the attraction.
During the first year, the experience was
soundtracked with a new score from composer
Gordon Goodwin, but by 2002, a new soundtrack
by John Debney, based on Danny Elfman's film
score, could be heard throughout the rooms.
The *Haunted Mansion Holiday* was such a success

that a version of the attraction premiered in
Tokyo Disneyland as the *Haunted Mansion Holiday
Nightmare*. The overlay was similar to that in
California, with many of the same elements,
including the custom gingerbread house in the
Grand Hall that changes each year. Both parks
offer special merchandise sold in honor of the
attraction and many fans visit the immersive
experience more than once over the holiday season.

As the fanbase of the film has grown, so has its
popularity in the parks—and vice versa.

"Millions of people a year go to Disneyland,"
Martens says. "If one of the signature attractions
in the park has a makeover based on this Tim
Burton film anybody who has not seen that
film goes home and watches it. People love

We Know Jack Podcast

Over the years, many of the crew members who worked on *Tim Burton's The Nightmare Before Christmas* have stayed in touch. The film remains a powerful touchpoint in their lives and careers all these years later. They've held reunions and crew parties, including for the 25th anniversary of the film, and some have continued to collaborate on other projects. But one of the most important documents of their continuing adoration for the movie is "We Know Jack," a podcast created in 2019 by production coordinator Kat Alioshin and set builder Todd Lookinland. Each episode focuses on one member of the *Nightmare* crew, reflecting back on what it was like to work in Skellington studio for two years.

"I can say, without hesitation, that I've never worked on a project before or since that was more exciting, more fun, or with everybody pulling in the same direction more," Lookinland says. "Everybody wanted to be there. With the podcast, we were trying to answer the questions of 'Why was this so magical? How do you recreate it? How come it's so hard to recreate a situation like this?' There's no real answer that we've found other than we were lucky. We were just super fortunate to have been involved in this thing that just turned out to be super fun, and super magical and super exciting."

"We Know Jack" features conversations with everyone from the film's editor Stan Webb to art director Deane Taylor to several of the animators, including Angie Glocka and Mike Belzer. The interviews are extremely detailed, with each participant sharing new behind-the-scenes stories and anecdotes about how the movie came together. It's a must-listen for any fan of the film.

"It's so fun to see people's reactions to hearing stories that they feel are very special and that they haven't heard before," Alioshin says. "And you wouldn't have heard them because they're coming from people's hearts. Someone we're interviewing will say 'I hadn't told anyone this before' and, to us, that is very cool."

Todd Lookinland and Kat Alioshin interview camera operator Pat Sweeney for the podcast.

We Know JACK

Top: The Oogie Boogie Bash at California Adventure Park; *Left: Haunted Mansion Holiday; Right:* Oogie Boogie greets guests at California Adventure Park.

the *Haunted Mansion*. They want to know the story of that attraction inside and out. They want to know anything that happens to it. Putting *The Nightmare Before Christmas* in that attraction puts *The Nightmare Before Christmas* into one of the most popular rides in the resort. And over the years, it has helped to turn *The Nightmare Before Christmas* into a Disney classic that today would be regarded as important to the Disney collection of films as any of the other animated films that are represented throughout the park."

Elsewhere in the parks, guests can meet Jack and Sally throughout the year. But it's really around Halloween when *Tim Burton's The Nightmare Before Christmas* takes over the various theme parks. The Oogie Boogie Bash, an annual Halloween party held at Disney California Adventure Park at Disneyland, debuted in 2019 as a replacement for Mickey's Halloween Party. The nighttime event, which runs on select evenings in September and October after normal park hours, is hosted by the bug-filled villain himself. Oogie Boogie is joined by numerous other villains, including the evil Queen from *Snow White and the Seven Dwarfs* (1937) and Ursula from *The Little Mermaid* (1989). The event features a parade, themed games, and live performances by parks

characters—villain and hero alike. Fans of all ages are encouraged to dress up in costume to trick-or-treat throughout the park.

Characters from *Nightmare* also appear at Mickey's Not-So-Scary Halloween Party at Walt Disney World in Florida, and Jack as Sandy Claws often pops up during annual events at Walt Disney World's *Haunted Mansion* and Disneyland Paris's *Phantom Manor*. Other popular events at the Disney Parks throughout the year include Halfway to Halloween, held in the spring leading up to May 4. All year, however, guests can don a pair of *Nightmare*-themed mouse ears featuring Sally's colorful patchwork design or an eerie bat with black-and-white pin stripes—perfect for evoking the holiday spirit in any month.

"*The Nightmare Before Christmas* has become the backbone of Disney's Halloween events," says Martens. "I think each year you start to see greater proliferation. If you go to Disney California Adventure any time from late September through the end of Halloween, the first thing you see when you walk into that gate is Oogie Boogie. You hear his voice echoing throughout the park. You hear his laughter. There is a huge hunger for *The Nightmare Before Christmas* among Disney theme park fans that continues to grow."

Each year, *Haunted Mansion Holiday* takes over *Haunted Mansion* in the Disney Parks.

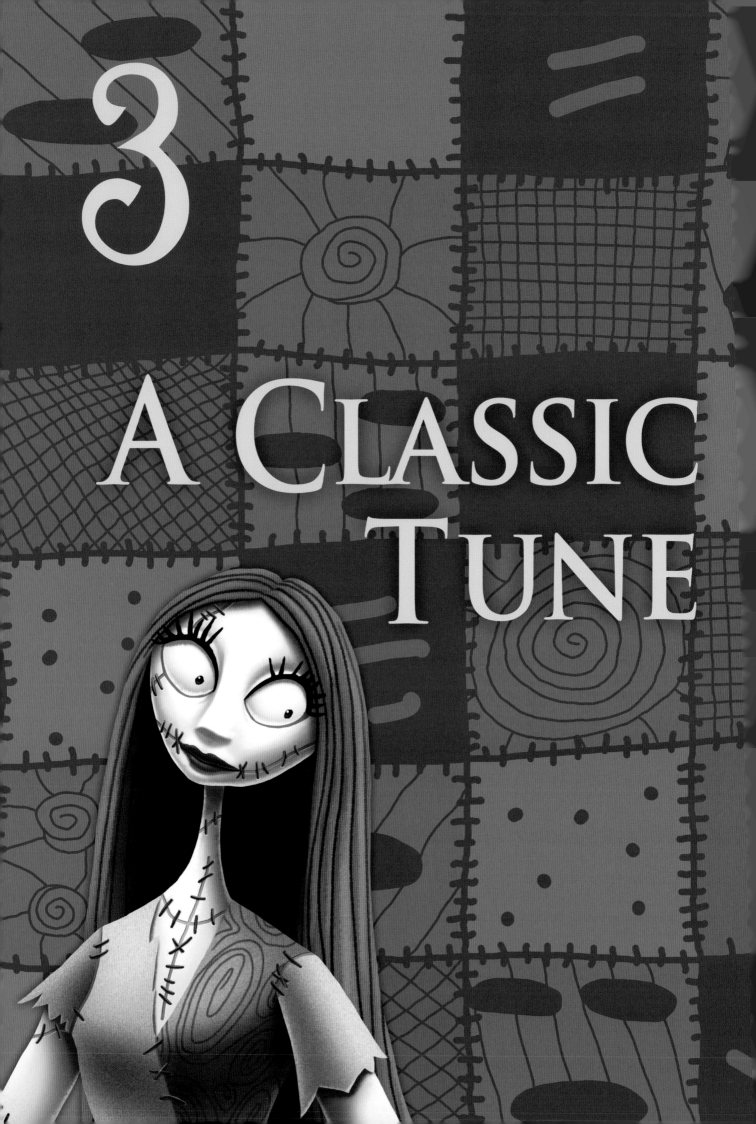

3

A Classic Tune

MUSIC AND SONGS

Tim Burton's The Nightmare Before Christmas wouldn't exist without its dynamic, quirky musical numbers and emotional score, which were written and composed by Danny Elfman, who was best known as the lead singer of American New Wave band Oingo Boingo before his foray into film scores. Burton had worked with Elfman several times prior to *Nightmare*, with their first collaboration being *Pee-wee's Big Adventure* in 1985. That film marked Burton's directorial debut and Elfman's first movie score, setting in motion a partnership that continues to this day. Elfman subsequently composed music for *Beetlejuice*, *Batman*, and *Edward Scissorhands* with Burton—as he also worked on projects for other filmmakers—but it was *Nightmare* that truly solidified the collaborative dynamic between the two.

Jack Skellington sings his way through Halloween Town.

When Burton began toying with the idea of adapting his poem *The Nightmare Before Christmas* into a feature-length film, he knew instinctually the story would be best told as a musical. The filmmaker approached Elfman with the concept, a few lyrical ideas, and some sketches, relying on Elfman to create songs that would reveal Jack's inner life and reflect the unique visual style of the stop-motion animation.

"Danny was one of the first people on board," Burton recalls. "He was doing music before there was a script. We would just talk about the story—I would say, 'This happens, that happens, and then that happens.' And he wrote an opera. It was a back-and-forth in that way. A lot of the script was developed based on the music. We had similar sensibilities and he was obviously like a character in it, so it was more organic. It wasn't, 'Here's the script, go.' He was instrumental in the development of the whole thing."

Elfman wrote the musical numbers and score cues that became the foundation of *Tim Burton's The Nightmare Before Christmas* and were used by screenwriter Caroline Thompson as a framework for the film's script. Neither Burton nor Elfman had ever written a musical, so there were no rules. Each song came naturally, with the pair focused simply on not becoming trapped by what was popular at the time.

"For both of us, our sense of rhyming and meter came from somewhere between Edward Gorey and Dr. Seuss," Elfman says. "That's probably where I get much of my lyrical rhyming and rhythm from. But we didn't have any idea of how to begin. We did have a clear idea of what we didn't want to do: 'We don't want this to sound like a Disney musical or Broadway musical.' Other than that, we didn't know what we wanted it to sound like."

Over the years, the music of *Tim Burton's The Nightmare Before Christmas* has generated its own legacy. By the late 1990s and early 2000s, the songs took on new shape with cover versions and re-releases of the original soundtrack. There was a clear connection between musical artists in the punk, emo, hard rock, and goth music scenes, especially in the 2000s, and mainstream bands like Fall Out Boy, Slipknot, and blink-182 paid homage to *Nightmare* with tattoos, song lyrics, and fashion choices. Walt Disney Records tapped numerous artists, from Korn to Evanescence's Amy Lee to Panic! at the Disco, to record official re-imaginings of the film's musical numbers. Elfman's lyrics spoke to a generation of introspective people who had grown up watching *Nightmare* as kids.

"Jack was this intellectual character who had all of these people in his community who loved and looked up to him, and yet he still felt like something was missing from his life," explains music journalist Rabab Al-Sharif. "He was looking for like a greater purpose. If you think about the themes in emo or hard rock music, it's very similar. It's about being misunderstood or longing for something more."

By the 2010s, Elfman's songs had fully established themselves in pop culture. Over the past decade, *Tim Burton's The Nightmare Before Christmas* has been performed live in concert in multiple countries, creating memorable moments of togetherness for fans. The songs continue to be reinterpreted by artists of all genres, and have become classics themselves. Because Elfman didn't lean on a particular style or trend when composing the music, *Nightmare*'s songs retain a timeless feel that holds up alongside Hollywood's best movie musicals.

"It's like a goth Rodgers and Hammerstein, with some jazz and blues mixed in," Al-Sharif says. "They could have made it rockier or gone in a different direction, like New Wave, but they didn't. They made it more like a traditional musical, with some unique quirks added in. I think that has helped it stay relevant for so long, because the songs don't ever feel outdated."

Elfman isn't exactly sure why the songs from the film have taken on a life of their own. "When Tim and I were creating them they were just a bunch of crazy, weird songs of a non-contemporary style," the songwriter says.

"My goal was to write songs that could be written now, but they also could have been written in the '30s or in the '50s. To try to make it so you can't even put an era behind it—that was my objective. I didn't want them to sound contemporary because at that point I really did not like what Broadway and contemporary musicals were doing musically. It bored me. So all I cared about is that it didn't go into that territory. But at the same time, I was drawing on all these different influences. I have no idea what keeps them alive, but I don't think any songwriter ever does."

DEVELOPING THE SONGS

After Burton approached Elfman about writing songs for a stop-motion feature version of *The Nightmare Before Christmas*, the musician dove in immediately. He began writing songs in 1991, working in tandem with Burton. Elfman was inspired by Burton's concept and found it relatively easy to write the melodies and lyrics that began to frame Jack's adventure. "He had all of these great pictures and drawings, as well as lines and poems; fragments of stuff," Elfman recalled. "I remember a number of times I pushed him out the door because I started hearing the songs in my head. I'd start right on that, and three days later I'd have a demo which I'd come back and play for him. Then we'd start the next part of the story."

The songs, composed by Elfman in a makeshift studio in screenwriter Caroline Thompson's Burbank house, came to life chronologically. Burton would recount part of the story, and then Elfman would write the next song. He wrote quickly because Selick and the crew had already begun to set up shop at Skellington studio in San Francisco. As he worked, Elfman drew on multiple influences for the music, pulling on past time periods and vintage styles. Kurt Weill's *The Threepenny Opera*, Cole Porter, Gilbert and Sullivan, and Rodgers and Hammerstein were the most significant inspirations.

Cab Calloway was a big inspiration for composer Danny Elfman.

Tim Burton and Danny Elfman in the recording studio.

"Town Meeting Song," with its casual, conversational singing-slash-talking charm, felt to Elfman like "the kind of thing Cole Porter might have done ages ago." For the lively number "What's This?," which Jack sings as he discovers Christmas Town, Elfman looked back to the Victorian era. "When I was writing 'What's This?' I was definitely thinking of Gilbert and Sullivan's 'I Am the Very Model,'" he says. "I wanted to write something that was a tongue twister. Quick, insistent, and tricky."

On "Oogie Boogie's Song," Elfman paid homage to Cab Calloway's 1931 song "Minnie The Moocher," which was performed in a 1932 Betty Boop cartoon of the same name (as well as other Calloway numbers). Notably, Oingo

Boingo had once covered the musician's bluesy tune in their 1982 film *Forbidden Zone*. For Elfman, Ken Page, known as a Broadway star, was the right singer to embody the swaggering villain's signature tune. "We auditioned a lot of Oogie Boogies," he notes. "And when I heard Ken I felt like, 'Oh my God, this is who I wrote it for.'"

At the time, Elfman was still in Oingo Boingo, his formative band, and he couldn't help but pull from his experience as the lead singer of a rock group. In fact, the film's opening number, "This Is Halloween," shares a lyric with an Oingo Boingo song, "Tender Lumplings." Many of Jack's musical moments drew on Elfman's own desires to begin the next chapter of his career.

"Even though it was clearly Tim's story, I was also telling my own story through Jack because it was very personal for me," Elfman says. "When you're the songwriter and lead singer in a band, you're the king of your own little world, your own little bubble, your universe. That's what you are, and I, very much at that point, wanted out of that. I wanted to get out of my band and I didn't know how to do it. I felt a lot of obligation and guilt. So as I was writing Jack's lyrics, even though I didn't contribute anything to the storyline, I was adding my own emotional sense to the character: Trying to find a way out of something that was hard to escape."

Alongside the musical numbers, Elfman penned the film's score. He wanted the score cues to echo or hint at the songs, a process that became a jigsaw puzzle for Elfman to solve. "I loved doing the score because it was such a challenge," he explains. "I'd never had something where I was really dealing with so many different thematic elements. But, for me, that's kind of heaven because I love writing in a narrative thematic way. So having so many melodies to work with was just a pleasure. Just diving in and out, knitting them all together. A big jigsaw puzzle. I just had so much fun doing that score."

As Elfman was writing, Henry Selick was preparing to shoot the first stop-motion scenes. The director was patiently awaiting demos of the music, so Elfman and Burton went into a recording studio for one very long night where Elfman recorded nearly every vocal part in the film.

"Recording the demos, Tim was like the producer and I was behind the glass in a small recording studio and we'd just go song by song, laying down all the voices," Elfman remembers. "At the end of that session we were talking and I said, 'Look, Tim, I don't know how to put this. But I really need to sing Jack.' And he goes,

'You'll sing the part, don't worry.' Originally, I didn't think of it as for me. But then as I got into Jack's character, I became so attached to it I simply found it impossible to give it up."

Once the film was cast, Elfman re-recorded the vocals and the songs with the rest of the actors. As with so much in the film's development, the voiceover work was intrinsically shaped by the cast members involved. In fact, Elfman ended up using several of his own original demo vocals in the final versions for Jack. For the bit parts, like the inhabitants of Halloween Town, Elfman assembled a small group of singers, including Greg Proops and Randy Crenshaw. No one was cast in a particular role; instead, Elfman wanted to improvise everything in the studio.

"It was just winging it song by song," he remembers. "It was really fun because it was a very talented group. And in that group, everybody could just switch and swap voices. It was all done in a very improvisational manner of who's doing what. Nothing was planned out going into the vocal sessions. And I knew that any voice that anybody else couldn't do I could do because I'd already done all the character voices on the demos."

Despite any challenges along the way, writing the music in *Tim Burton's The Nightmare Before Christmas* felt almost effortless for Elfman. He credits Burton for some of the favorite lyrics in the film, including a quip about finding a head in the lake during "Town Meeting Song," as well as the feeling that there were no creative restrictions or boundaries.

"The initial creation part was about the simplest thing I've ever done," Elfman recalls of the film's music. "Over the years I've had things that were really a struggle and still turn out good and I love them. And there are certain things here and there that just seem to come together quickly, simply, and without effort, and *Nightmare* was one of those. Going through Tim, channeling through me, into these songs."

MUSICAL LEGACY

Like the film itself, the original soundtrack to *Tim Burton's The Nightmare Before Christmas*, released October 12, 1993, was not a massive mainstream hit. Although Danny Elfman's work was nominated for the Golden Globe for Best Original Score, the album peaked at No. 64 on the *Billboard* Top 200 chart and then quickly lost momentum. Although the music was one of the film's most memorable aspects, it seemed doomed to fall by the cultural wayside as the movie had. But as *Nightmare* picked up speed thanks to its growing fan base and frequent home video and theatrical re-releases, its songs gained a similarly impassioned following, who have continued to celebrate the beloved tunes.

As the original songs have captivated music fans over the years, many reinterpretations have also emerged. To coincide with the film's 2006 re-release in Disney Digital 3D, Walt Disney Records unveiled a special edition of the soundtrack featuring a bonus disc with covers by five popular artists: Fall Out Boy, Panic! at the Disco, Marilyn Manson, Fiona Apple, and She Wants Revenge. The special edition release of the film's soundtrack was so successful that two years later, around the film's fifteenth anniversary, the record label decided to create an entire covers album of Elfman's songs, dubbed *Nightmare Revisited*. The album featured twenty total tracks, including both the film's musical numbers and its score cues. Walt Disney Records enlisted a vast range of musicians for the project, from Plain White T's to The Polyphonic Spree to Rise Against.

"I wanted to literally reinvent and revisit this whole soundtrack," explains Dani Markman, A&R at Walt Disney Records, who helmed the album alongside Tom MacDougall. "It was fairly daunting because there were quite a few tracks. I wanted it to seem truthful and organic to the property, so it wasn't just about who I was liking at that moment and who was popular—it was really about who was right for the track. I felt like overall *Nightmare*

Top: The film's soundtrack; *Middle:* Fall Out Boy; *Bottom:* Plain White T's.

Top: Nightmare Revisited; *Middle:* Rise Against; *Bottom:* Korn.

Revisited was going to be a darker release. I really didn't want it to feel like it was pop in any way. What came together, magically, is a perfect amalgam of the best of all of these interesting, remarkable musicians that shared as much passion as I did about this music."

Markman felt that Amy Lee, the singer of rock band Evanescence, was the best possible choice to reimagine "Sally's Song," and that Korn, who covered "Kidnap the Sandy Claws," was an inevitable inclusion. But not all of the artists were household names, especially those Markman and MacDougall recruited for the instrumental score cues. Icelandic group amiina recorded a new rendition of "Doctor Finkelstein/In the Forest" while tribute band Vitamin String Quartet offered their version of "Jack and Sally Montage." The aim was for each artist to personalize a particular song in their own style.

"I gave them full rein," Markman notes. "Tom and I were there for our respective artists to give some feedback, but for the most part we really didn't need to because the tracks were all pretty great. And we let them hire whoever they wanted. We told them, 'This is what we can afford to give you and all we ask is that you deliver a great track to us.'"

While participating in *Nightmare Revisited* was an unequivocal yes for everyone involved, the process was not without its hurdles. Many of the artists found it nearly impossible to translate Elfman's musical score into pop or rock music. It was surprising just how complicated the arrangements actually were, which proved daunting in the recording studio. Chicago punk band Rise Against covered "Making Christmas," a feat so challenging frontman Tim McIlrath says the group has never played the song since they initially recorded it.

"I don't remember any creative guidelines," McIlrath recalls. "If there were, we ignored them. We got the offer, we

Reinterpreting "Sally's Song"

When Caroline Thompson first came onboard to write the screenplay for the film, Sally wasn't as significant as she is in the final version. As the character evolved thanks to Thompson's conception of the rag doll, so did her importance to the story. Sally's big moment in the spotlight came with "Sally's Song," where she worries about Jack's desire to take over Christmas.

Like with "Jack's Lament," for "Sally's Song" Elfman drew on classic Hollywood musicals, as well as Kurt Weill and the sound of Berlin in the 1930s. Ultimately, though, the song reflects the heroine herself. "The song was really just inspired by the character in Tim's description of her," Elfman recalls. "It was very simple, and he felt and I felt that her song should also be very simple, with just the emotions that she was feeling."

For the film, actress Catherine O'Hara sang "Sally's Song," a plaintive ballad that lasts less than two minutes. The scene was animated by Trey Thomas, who drew his inspiration from O'Hara's vocals. "I think that's a beautiful little performance," the animator notes of O'Hara's contribution. "It's this delicate, little, shaky, frail thing that I just loved."

"The song itself is beautiful," O'Hara adds, reflecting on what she wanted to convey. "But Sally's concern for Jack's welfare along with her powerful yearning to be seen by him is something too many of us know all too well."

Over the years, more and more singers have offered their own versions of "Sally's Song." Fiona Apple and Amy Lee recorded renditions of the song for the Walt Disney Records official covers

Billie Eilish performs as Sally in Los Angeles in 2021.

Helena Bonham Carter performs "Sally's Song" at Royal Albert Hall in 2013;
Inset: Sally singing in the film.

albums, each imbuing the track with a uniquely memorable performance. "*The Nightmare Before Christmas* is my number one biggest influence artistically in every way," Lee told *SPIN*. "[When I was young] I literally would sit in my bedroom and sing 'Sally's Song,' or in the car driving to school. The best part about it [recording the song] was that I had no restrictions or direction or anything. I picked the producer, who's a friend, and we just made the song however we wanted together."

For the German version of the film's soundtrack, singer Nina Hagen infused the character's song with an ethereal pop sensibility, while a raucous punk rendition by Scott Murphy appeared on the Japanese edition of *Nightmare Revisited*. On October 7, 2013, Helena Bonham Carter embodied Sally for a theatrical rendition of the tune at London's Royal Albert Hall as part of the world premiere of "Danny Elfman's Music From the Films of Tim Burton." The actress was accompanied by John Mauceri leading the BBC Concert Orchestra, and the event marked one of the first times Elfman's songs from *Tim Burton's The Nightmare Before Christmas* were showcased during a live event. In the years since, O'Hara has revisited the song, as has Billie Eilish, who performed as Sally on stage in Los Angeles in 2021.

jumped on it, and we got a deadline. We were making a record at the time and we were in the studio in Chicago, at a studio called Gravity Studios in Wicker Park. We were so focused on the album that we were thinking, 'This will just be a fun cover song and we'll knock it out.' And I remember us being totally wrong. We started really listening to the song and we realized, 'Holy shit, these arrangements are psychotic. How are we going to make this happen?' We really had to pop the hood on that song. It was one of the more challenging things we've ever had to play or record."

Plain White T's, who covered "Poor Jack," asked the record label for Elfman's musical score sheets to help translate the song for a band. To reimagine the song, bassist Mike Retondo learned all of the score parts on acoustic guitar and bass and then recorded each part one by one to layer over each other. "It was a weird, weird musical thing that was very much outside of our wheelhouse," he remembers. "It's not a pop song, so for band members slinging electric guitars it was a big jump."

The final version, which Plain White T's have also never played live, is comprised of Retondo and singer Tom Higgenson, who wanted to bring a sense of theatricality to the cover. "That was a challenge," Higgenson says. "Because the way Jack sings in the movie, the songs are in the key of speech. He's almost talking it and then singing a little bit here and there. We agreed to it thinking, 'Oh yeah, that'll be awesome.' And then when it came time to actually do it we were like, 'What did we sign up for? How are we going to do this?' Luckily, Mike is a really exceptional musician and instrumentalist. He did all the heavy lifting."

Korn frontman Jonathan Davis was a longtime fan of the film when the band was brought on to cover "Kidnap the Sandy Claws" and he had been collecting its merchandise for years prior.

Although Korn has also never performed the cover since recording it, Davis did join Elfman onstage for a special rendition with the Metropolitan Camerata Orchestra in Mexico City in 2017. That performance exemplified what Davis wanted to bring to the version on *Nightmare Revisited*.

"It was one thing for a band to do a rock cover, but I wanted it to allude to the theater, like being on stage," Davis explains. "That was my intention when singing it, and that's why the way I projected it and the way I did my voice was with a long enunciated, very dramatic delivery. I wanted it to feel like how it felt when you watched the movie—a big theatrical production. Even though it's animated, it just feels like it should be on a stage, belting out to the masses."

For Elfman, it was gratifying to see so many different artists connecting to his work. "It was just cool," he says. "These songs get into the heads of so many different people. I loved the

Korn singer Jonathan Davis with Danny Elfman.

Reinterpretations of the film's music have included lullabies for young children.

fact that it was such a wide variety of artists. The whole thing was just wonderful for me because *Nightmare*, when it came out, was so misunderstood."

Nightmare Revisited peaked at No. 31 on the *Billboard* Top 200 chart, but hit No. 1 on the *Billboard* Top Compilation Albums chart. The success of *Nightmare Revisited* led to Walt Disney Records creating similar compilation albums for future Burton movies *Alice In Wonderland* and *Frankenweenie*. *Almost Alice*, featuring artists like The Cure's Robert Smith and Scottish rock band Franz Ferdinand, came out in 2010, while *Frankenweenie Unleashed!*, released in 2012, showcased original songs and covers by the likes of Imagine Dragons, Karen O, and Plain White T's. The record label also compiled *Avengers Assemble*, around 2012's Marvel Studios film *The Avengers*, and *Muppets: The Green Album*, a collection of Muppets-inspired covers, in 2011. It was clear with *Nightmare Revisited* that fans were interested in the various ways classic film songs could be reworked, particularly those that felt too edgy for a mass audience.

"When somebody who is more mainstream covers a song that may have been less palatable to the mainstream and puts it into a language that a wider audience can understand, that's when people discover more obscure songs," McIlrath reflects. "It gets a new life and it regenerates itself. For someone to give these songs, that were just meant to be played by a symphony with the actors' voices, to Amy Lee from Evanescence, or whoever, it's like, 'Oh, I understand this now.'"

Unsurprisingly, Elfman's songs from *Tim Burton's The Nightmare Before Christmas* translate well to instrumental music—perhaps more easily than to rock or pop. In 2020, Markman tapped pianist Chantry Johnson to record a collection of *Nightmare* lullabies for infants titled *Little Nightmares: Soothing Piano Renditions*. The album featured eleven tracks, including soothing versions of "What's This?" and "Poor Jack."

"Today, you can walk around Disneyland and you see babies in Jack Skellington onesies," Markman says. "I'm such a fan of the film that for years I wanted to make a lullaby album based on the music because I thought it was melodically so perfect. We made it for hipster parents to play sweet lullaby versions of the songs to their children. I wanted to call it *Baby Nightmares*, but the marketing team was appalled. I didn't want over-the-top arrangements or for it to sound like a music box, because then it just skews in one direction just for babies. Whereas, if you have nice piano arrangements other fans can enjoy it too."

Elfman himself has continued to breathe new life into the songs. To celebrate the twenty-fifth anniversary of their partnership, Elfman and Burton released *The Danny Elfman & Tim Burton 25th Anniversary Music Box* in 2010. The expansive collection, which included sixteen CDs and a DVD in a limited edition zoetrope box, showcased music from *Tim Burton's The Nightmare Before Christmas*, as well as films like *Edward Scissorhands*, *Batman*, and *Sleepy Hollow*. Warner Bros sold an exclusive limited number of

An elaborate box set celebrating the music of Tim Burton and Danny Elfman.

one thousand box sets in total, making it a highly sought-after collectible.

The CDs featured the songs and scores known and loved by the fans, but the most exciting inclusion was the unheard tracks and demos Elfman created while writing for *Nightmare*. An unused song from the film, "This Time," sung by Elfman, emerged alongside rough demos. Pulling the box set together was a massive task for Elfman's agents Richard Kraft and Laura Engel, largely because Elfman hadn't catalogued any of his material. In fact, Kraft ended up searching through garbage bags full of cassette tapes in Elfman's garage to compile the tracks for the box set.

"We dug up archival stuff from *The Nightmare Before Christmas*—a lot of Danny's original demos and a lot of underscore that was never on the soundtrack," Kraft recalls. "It was such a nerd spectacular. For instance, in 'What's This?' there's

a moment where some elves cross the screen and sing 'La, la, la, la' as a counterpoint. I read message boards of nerds and they were always complaining that the elf choir was not included on the original soundtrack. So I went and found that track and added it to the background of the song. Finally, the elves could be heard."

Contemporary artists continue to cover the songs from *Tim Burton's The Nightmare Before Christmas*. In 2020, Disney's official a cappella group DCappella released "The Nightmare Before Christmas Medley" to celebrate Halloween. The following Halloween, in 2021, indie rock duo Larkin Poe showcased an instrumental cover of "Sally's Song" performed on slide guitar, and later that year Matt Heafy, lead singer of metal band Trivium, dropped a heavy, electric-guitar driven rendition of "Jack's Lament." For DCapella member Joe Santoni, the medley was an opportunity to pay tribute to Elfman's work by giving it a new spin.

Blink-182's "I Miss You"

In 2003, fans buzzed with excitement as blink-182 sang about Jack and Sally's enduring love in the emo-tinged single "I Miss You," which appeared on the band's fifth studio album, *blink-182*. Co-written by guitarist Tom DeLonge and bassist Mark Hoppus and produced by Jerry Finn, the acoustic song was inspired by The Cure's 1983 track "The Love Cats," as well as *Tim Burton's The Nightmare Before Christmas*. It was officially released as a single on February 2, 2004, just in time for Valentine's Day, and went on to be certified gold. Originally, it was drummer Travis Barker's idea to reference Burton's work.

"It was Travis's idea to include the Jack and Sally reference in 'I Miss You,'" Hoppus remembers. "We were writing a song with dark lyrics about love and Travis said, 'What about *The Nightmare Before Christmas*?' For our generation, *The Nightmare Before Christmas* was such a huge movie not only in its aesthetic, but in its themes, its production design, and music."

Although the song's music video, directed by Jonas Auckerland, doesn't directly reference the film, it is set in a haunted manor, with shots of a graveyard and supernatural elements. The band filmed the video in an old mansion overlooking Hollywood with the intention of creating something "Gothic and dark and weird." In the years since its release, the song has been covered by numerous artists, including 5 Seconds of Summer, and inspired The Chainsmokers' 2016 single "Closer." It marked a turning point for blink-182, as well as a key touchpoint for fans of Jack and Sally.

"'I Miss You' is an important song for blink-182 because it was such a departure from anything we had done prior to that point," Hoppus says. "We wrote it in a rented house in Rancho Santa Fe on acoustic guitars and it came together in a very special, magical way. It's one of the highlights of the album."

Mark Hoppus, Tom DeLonge, and Travis Barker of blink-182.

"To me, personally, recording our *Nightmare Before Christmas* medley was one of my favorite DCappella projects," says Santoni. "I'm our resident Halloween fanatic—I was born on Halloween—and this movie and Danny Elfman's unforgettable soundtrack has always been one of my favorites. So to have the opportunity to really dig into the score and learn our individual parts was such a blast. Like everything DCappella does, I hope that when people hear our arrangement, they hear something new and different, but that we still managed to capture the wonderfully strange and peculiar elements of Elfman's original soundtrack."

For Davis, *Tim Burton's The Nightmare Before Christmas* continues to resonate thanks in part to the music. "It is an amazing musical story that touches on the child in all of us," the Korn singer says. "It's this weird, twisted Christmas-Halloween collaboration and that's what so special—combining the magic of those two holidays. It all comes down to the amazing characters that Tim came up with, and how Danny brought them to life with his music, and then the actual artists that performed and voiced them. It was all a perfect mix the way it came together."

An album of music inspired by the *Haunted Mansion Holiday*.

LIVE PERFORMANCES

The energetic theatricality of the music in *Tim Burton's The Nightmare Before Christmas* allows the songs to translate seamlessly to a live performance. In fact, the first time Danny Elfman performed a song from the film onstage was prior to its release at an exhibition for movie theater owners in Las Vegas. Elfman sang a rendition of "What's This?" for the crowd, who gathered in the summer of 1993 to learn about upcoming releases. The musician received a perplexed reaction. "I would describe the reaction as a bit like staring into the eye of a chicken," recalls Richard Kraft, Elfman's co-manager and agent who has also produced many of the live *Nightmare* shows. "It was perfect that the song was called 'What's This?' because the exhibitors were asking themselves the same question. In no way did it give me any peace of mind that things were going to go well."

"I was so nervous I blacked it out of my memory," Elfman adds of the performance. "I sang to a track and I think it went horribly. Technically I was performing it live, but it wasn't like performing it on stage."

After the film came out, Elfman left his band, Oingo Boingo, who played their final show at the Universal Amphitheatre on Halloween night in 1995. Once the band had said farewell, Elfman moved on to score films like *Mission: Impossible* (1996), *Good Will Hunting* (1997), and Burton's *Sleepy Hollow* (1999). He didn't return to the stage as a singer, although Elfman continued to appear at various live events in support of *Tim Burton's The Nightmare Before Christmas*. Two decades after the movie's release, things changed unexpectedly for the musician, who re-discovered his love for performing live thanks to his ongoing collaboration with Burton.

After Elfman and Burton celebrated their twenty-fifth year of working together with the collectible box set in 2011, the team put together a concert at Royal Albert Hall in London two years later. Initially, it was intended as an instrumental symphony performance conducted by John Mauceri, but late in the planning process Kraft convinced Elfman to go on stage

Paul Reubens, Catherine O'Hara, and Danny Elfman reprise their characters live onstage in 2015.

as Jack. "We got the booking and there was no show," Kraft remembers. "So there was a mad scramble to put together an evening of music from their collaboration. The idea was, 'Why doesn't it culminate with Danny singing some songs from *The Nightmare Before Christmas*?' Which presented an interesting quandary because Danny had not really performed onstage for around eighteen years."

"At that point it was almost eighteen years since I'd sung publicly," Elfman says. "That's a big break. I didn't know if I could do it. I had a lot of stage fright my whole life—it actually never got better. When I retired from performing in '95, I didn't miss it. Even though I missed the energy of the shows, I didn't miss the hell I went through psychologically walking out on stage in front of an audience, which was incredibly difficult for me."

Standing backstage at Royal Albert Hall, Elfman froze. But in the wings behind him was Helena Bonham Carter, preparing to sing "Sally's Song." The actress encouraged Elfman out onto the stage and, in that moment, his career changed completely. "It was really one of the big emotional experiences of my life," he recalls. "Because I

really had to push past this wall and go out there. I had absolutely no idea what to expect. I was prepared for the worst, but I was astonished by the wonderful, warm response. It was a great experience doing Jack live for the first time. To this day, that performance—doing Jack live—was, and still is, one of the greatest nights of my life."

The response was so strong and the concert so lauded that Elfman and Kraft began to consider the idea of doing an entire live concert of *Tim Burton's The Nightmare Before Christmas*. To test it, Elfman first brought a production to Tokyo in 2015 and performed most of the vocals himself. It was immediately successful, which led the team to discuss where to bring the show next. "We were at a restaurant in Tokyo and the Danny said, 'That was interesting. Why don't we do it at the Hollywood Bowl?'" Kraft recounts. "And we said, 'Great, that gives us a year and a half to get it together.' Because it was something we wanted to do around Halloween. And he said, 'No, I meant this year.'"

"*The Nightmare Before Christmas* Live at the Hollywood Bowl" debuted on Halloween night in 2015. Elfman returned to voice Jack, with an

orchestra again conducted by Mauceri. Ken Page and Catherine O'Hara reprised their film roles of Oogie Boogie and Sally, and Paul Reubens made a surprise appearance for a rendition of Lock, Shock, and Barrel's "Kidnap the Sandy Claws." Elfman concluded the evening with a performance of Oingo Boingo's "Dead Man's Party" with his former bandmate Steve Bartek.

Since then, "*The Nightmare Before Christmas* Live at the Hollywood Bowl" has returned several times, in 2016, 2018, and 2019. The cast has reprised their roles at subsequent shows, some of which have featured live projections by creative studio Mousetrappe on the iconic arch of the Hollywood Bowl. Each performance has been bigger and more elaborate—and every show has sold out. For the cast members, the performances have revealed how expansive the fan base of *Tim Burton's The Nightmare Before Christmas* has truly become.

"That's when I really began to understand the following for the film and the whole experience of it," Page says. "Because until you see everybody in one place, you go, 'Yeah, okay, people like it.' The concerts are where you really understand not only the fan base, but also the art form that the film really is projecting on these huge screens. And it's a very unique experience because people not only get to see us live in front of them, they also see the technical art form of doing voiceover work for a film. I've been floored by the reaction that I get."

"It's really exciting," Reubens adds. "I felt like the audience was really excited I was there and they loved the music and they loved the movie and you could feel that. It has practically become a yearly thing and is really fun."

For O'Hara, returning to the stage as Sally has been nerve-wracking, but also very rewarding. "It has been really exciting to sing a beautiful song with a beautiful orchestra in front of thousands of people who just want me to be Sally," the actress says. "I was scared before each performance because I hadn't sung the song for over twenty years and I was expected to sing it in the original key. I had a few voice lessons and practiced a lot

at home. It's a very tricky song to sing, though the final effect needs to feel pure and simple. It really helped that the movie was playing behind me on the big screen and I hoped the audience was focused on that real Sally while I sang."

In 2020, due to the COVID-19 pandemic, live performances became impossible. That year, several Broadway actors came together for a virtual benefit concert of the film's music in partnership with Elfman, Burton, and Disney Music Group. The one-night event, held on Halloween, was live-streamed for audiences around the world. It was directed by actor James Monroe Iglehart, who also performed as Oogie Boogie, and featured Rafael Casal as Jack, Adrienne Warren as Sally, Nik Walker as Lock, Lesli Margherita as Shock, Rob McClure as Barrel, and Danny Burstein as the narrator. Proceeds from the concert benefited the Lymphoma Research Foundation and The Actors Fund, which supported out-of-work stage actors during the pandemic shutdown.

"We spent no money," Iglehart explained of the virtual show's DIY quality. "Everything you see, everything you'll see in this concert is from people's houses. We're wearing scarves, we're wearing sunglasses, we're wearing wigs, we've got kitchen utensils just to tell a story—like an old-school way of telling a story."

As the world began to reopen in 2021, Elfman and Kraft wanted to devise a way to bring *Tim Burton's The Nightmare Before Christmas* back to the stage. For two nights, over Halloween weekend, *Tim Burton's The Nightmare Before Christmas Live-To-Film Concert* took over the Banc of California Stadium in Los Angeles. O'Hara was unavailable due to her filming schedule, so the team invited Billie Eilish to stand in as Sally and "Weird Al" Yankovic to perform as Shock. Elfman, Page, and Reubens voiced their onscreen roles, with Page receiving the biggest standing ovation of the evening when he came out as Oogie Boogie. To create a more immersive experience, Kraft brought in a sixteen-foot-tall Jack Skellington puppet that was originally made for the Disney Parks. Elfman

Jack Skellington was an important part of Elfman's Coachella set in 2022.

wrote new narration for Jack, which was recorded and programmed for the puppet, who emerged repeatedly throughout the concert.

Elfman has continued to showcase the music of the film outside of the United States, as well. The musician held a series of three concerts, "*The Nightmare Before Christmas* Live in Tokyo," at the Tokyo International Forum in the spring of 2019, and later that year "*Tim Burton's The Nightmare Before Christmas* Live in Concert" came to London's OVO Arena Wembley for two nights in December. Page and O'Hara, as well as Mauceri, flew to England to perform at the events. Elfman returned to the London venue in December of 2022 for a rendition of *Nightmare*'s songs synced to the film, accompanied by the BBC Concert Orchestra and joined by Phoebe Bridgers as Sally and original cast member Ken Page.

While most of the live events have involved a screening of the film projected behind the musical performance, Elfman has more recently toyed

with other formats. In the spring of 2022, Elfman took the stage at the popular Coachella Valley Music and Arts Festival, performing a showcase of his musical career. Initially booked as part of the festival's lineup in 2020, the performance was delayed for two years due to the pandemic, allowing Elfman and his team more time to conceptualize the best possible sixty-minute set. The set included an array of the songwriter's film contributions, as well as songs from Oingo Boingo and his 2021 solo studio album, *Big Mess*. To celebrate *Tim Burton's The Nightmare Before Christmas* Elfman created a new mash-up of "Jack's Lament," "This Is Halloween," and "What's This?"

"That was the second-weirdest thing I've ever done in my life," Elfman says. "There was no way to know if or how it was going to work. There was no take it out of town and try it out. It just does not make sense performing 'Jack's Lament' next to an Oingo Boingo song and a *Big Mess* song that is all feedback. I thought I was walking out into a train

Danny Elfman performs at Coachella in 2022.

wreck of my own design. That was the feeling I had going into Coachella. It was a crazy concept show to create an illogical mishmash of elements and styles that had virtually no relationship to each other, which is the nonsensical, schizophrenic story of my life."

The reaction from fans and the press, however, was immense. Between the first and second weekend of the festival, Elfman's audience multiplied significantly thanks to word of mouth and social media. Engel, who has managed Elfman since his Oingo Boingo days and produced the Coachella performance alongside the musician, wasn't surprised.

"He overdelivered beyond anyone's expectations with that performance and the setlist and the way he put it together," she says. "There was an incredible team that worked on it to make it so great, but the creative vision of everything begins and ends with Danny. Danny's music has impacted many generations, but *Nightmare* is something that people saw when

they were little *kids*, then again as teenagers, in college, as adults, and then as parents with their kids. A lot of people said they only came to Coachella to see Danny."

For Elfman, these live performances affirm the legacy of *Tim Burton's The Nightmare Before Christmas*. The ongoing enthusiastic response helps to ease the initial pain he felt when the film disappeared after its theatrical release. The film and its music were revived beyond anyone's wildest dreams.

"Of everything I'd worked on at that point, if I could pick the one thing that I could wish a second life on, it was *Nightmare*," Elfman reflects. "Because I've worked on plenty of movies that failed. Probably the majority. But on very rare occasions, there are films that don't do that well but then maintain the life on their own afterwards. If you would have told me I'd be doing *Nightmare* live on stage and I'd have sold out eight shows at the Hollywood Bowl, I would have said you were insane. But here we are."

Over the years, the film's music has been
celebrated through live concerts and
performances in the US and beyond.

4
WHAT'S THIS?

MERCHANDISE, GAMES, AND ODDITIES

Over time, *Tim Burton's The Nightmare Before Christmas* has become so ubiquitous in pop culture that it can seem almost impossible to go a day without seeing Jack Skellington's face. The dapper king of Halloween is emblazoned on T-shirts and hats, printed onto yoga leggings, and even found on infant onesies. He's a daily inspiration in the lives of many fans, both in their homes as toys and décor and on their bodies as fashion. While themed merchandise has been available since *Nightmare* opened in theaters in 1993, the volume and variety has increased year by year. In fact, it continues to grow in a way that is almost unparalleled in Hollywood. It's fair to say that a portion of *Nightmare*'s success is due to this constant surge of product, all of which is seen and sanctioned by Tim Burton before it hits stores.

"Merchandising has arguably been as crucial to the success of *The Nightmare Before Christmas* as it has been to *Star Wars*," explains Lisa Morton, author of *Trick or Treat: A History of Halloween*. "*Nightmare* benefited from the power of a marketing behemoth behind it, and they took advantage of it early on, although it was increased exponentially over the years. I'm astonished at seeing ads now for things like *Nightmare* cuckoo clocks. The film's original release in 1993 also coincided with the rise of Halloween collectibles, so it provided a new tsunami of delightful collectibles that were more affordable than many of the sought-after vintage pieces."

Initially, the merchandise available for fans of *Tim Burton's The Nightmare Before Christmas* was relatively limited. While it was possible for fans of the film to bring the characters home after seeing *Nightmare* in theaters, like with *Star Wars* in 1977 there simply wasn't enough product available in stores. "*Nightmare*'s merchandising remains one of the few cases in which initial demand actually exceeded the amount of material available," Morton noted in her book. In fact, Disney wasn't sure what the best strategy was to market *Nightmare* toys.

"It was really hit-or-miss that first wave of merchandise," Selick says. "There was not a whole lot. It was like, 'What's the game plan here?' I think people were a little leery."

As *Tim Burton's The Nightmare Before Christmas* has grown in popularity so has the amount of merchandise. The strategy behind the scenes at Disney Parks, Experiences and Products, which licenses the film to various retailers, is fan-first. As there is more demand from the fans, more items become available. This has occurred with increasing force in the past decade. Since the late 2010s, the film has transitioned from a niche brand sold in fan-centric shops like Hot Topic to a brand supported by mass retailers like Wal-Mart.

A plethora of merchandise has been created to promote the film since its release.

Above: Sally and Jack plushes on display at the El Capitan Theatre in Los Angeles; *Inset:* Jack Skellington-inspired Mickey Mouse ears.

The film's merchandising shifted from a seasonal business, centered around Halloween and Christmas, to being a year-round property. Today, the products are intended to serve both the core audience, who have followed *Nightmare* since its inception, and those who have joined the Halloween Town crew more recently.

"People want it all," says Elise Barkan, Director of Global Franchise Development & Marketing at Disney Parks, Experiences and Products. "And from luggage to luxury, we do it all. However you want to express yourself, we absolutely love that. The beauty of our team is that we marry what the trend is now with the classic artwork and find ways to bring that to life for the consumer."

For Barkan, the goal is to create merchandise and consumer experiences that embrace the aesthetic and themes of the film. Burton's original drawings remain at the core of each piece of apparel, each toy, and each collectible because that visual storytelling is what makes the

merchandise so memorable. The aim isn't to create mainstream products that appeal to just anyone; instead, the design teams want to infuse the merchandise with the same sense of uniqueness as the film itself.

"The artistry in Tim Burton's work, and this film in particular, was disruptive," Barkan explains. "And there's something about positive disruption that sticks with people. The story is unexpected—it turns everything on its ear. It just lets people's imaginations flourish. It's like, 'Oh, I never thought about Halloween and Christmas this way.'"

Although Jack Skellington has always been the visual signifier of *Tim Burton's The Nightmare Before Christmas*, over the years Sally has become just as popular with consumers. Nowadays, fans can find most of the film's characters and sets—and even small details like the beloved Deadly Nightshade jar—as the inspiration for toys, games, clothing, and more. Ultimately, though, Jack and Sally remain the fan favorites.

Figurines, dolls, and accessories are popular merchandise items; *Opposite:* The highly sought-after "12 Faces of Jack."

"It's the eternal love story," Terrell Gentry, Senior Manager of Design at Disney Parks, Experiences and Products, explains. "I've worked on a lot of products for various franchises, and usually you have the main hero who is very popular, but I would say consumers really like Jack and Sally equally. We create a lot of items of Sally by herself, a lot of items with Jack by himself, and a lot of products with them together. The only other set of characters I could put on that same level would be Mickey and Minnie."

These days, Burton sees every toy and every T-shirt that gets designed. The filmmaker wants to ensure that anything inspired by *Tim Burton's The Nightmare Before Christmas* embraces his vision and stays true to what the fans originally loved about the story and its characters. Sometimes he says "No" to particular ideas or designs, and other times he offers a little sketch to guide a design concept. For Burton, it's miraculous to see Jack's face everywhere he goes. "I see Jack almost every day," Burton says. "It's incredible. That's the most shocking thing, but it makes me feel better than almost anything. It's a connection that I just feel very emotional and amazed about."

TOYS, COLLECTIBLES, AND DÉCOR

When the film was released in theaters in October of 1993, there wasn't nearly as much merchandise available as there would be just a few decades later. The original style guide for licensees— the companies contracted by Disney Parks, Experiences and Products to design, manufacture, and distribute themed products—was created with the help of the filmmakers, including Rick Heinrichs. From the very beginning, the goal was to capture the visual aesthetic and thematic essence of the film and its characters in any toys, dolls, or other merchandise without compromising Burton's original vision. A Jack doll needed to evoke the Jack that audiences saw on the screen, even if he was not an exact replica. Similarly, a mug or T-shirt should feel true to the film itself, acting as an extension of the story and the world.

Heinrichs, who hired several of the film's crew to help create the so-called "Design Bible," spent a lot of time finessing the concept art to ensure any toys or action figures would be of the best possible quality. Jack, with his long, thin limbs, was the most difficult character to translate from the screen into a consumer product. Despite these challenges, Heinrichs endeavored to keep a connection with the film itself—a sensibility and goal that continues to drive the design and creation of toys themed around *Tim Burton's The Nightmare Before Christmas*.

In late 1993, available products included T-shirts, mugs, buttons, Christmas ornaments, dolls, and stationery. A popular collectible, sold by Disney Art Editions and signed by Burton, was the "12 Faces of Jack," which featured twelve Jack Skellington heads with different facial expressions. Only 275 were created in total and the item has

since become a coveted piece, with sets selling for thousands of dollars in online auctions in recent years. The primary items that hit store shelves were action figures. The initial run of action figures by Hasbro included the Werewolf, the Behemoth, The Mayor, a glow-in-the-dark Oogie Boogie, Sandy Claws, the Evil Scientist, Sally, two versions of Jack—the Pumpkin King and Santa Jack—and a trio set of Lock, Shock, and Barrel. Each was packaged with a custom accessory, including a purse for Sally and a megaphone for The Mayor. Hasbro also released larger sixteen-inch Jack and Sally dolls, a Sandy Claws hand puppet, and an Oogie Boogie plush doll filled with bugs.

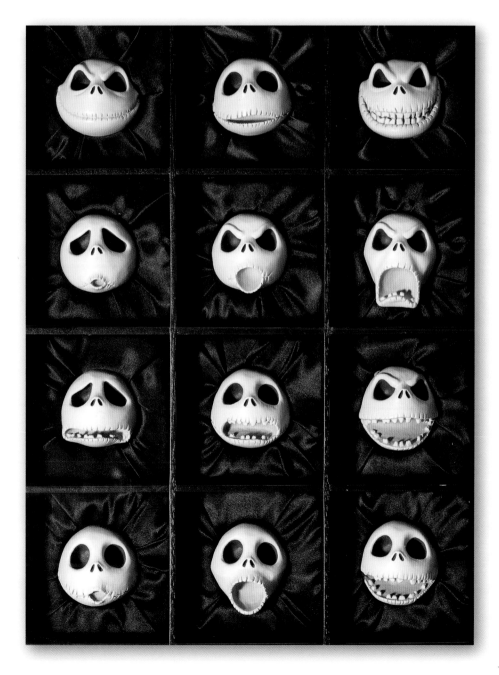

While other family films of the early 1990s, like *The Little Mermaid* and *The Lion King* (1994), were accompanied by a flood of merchandising tie-ins from McDonald's Happy Meal toys to Barbies, *Tim Burton's The Nightmare Before Christmas* wasn't so prolific. In fact, one of the only branded tie-ins was a collection of colorful, plastic watches that were part of a Burger King promotion in the fall of 1993. The watches were available for a mere $1.99 along with the purchase of a value meal at the fast food joint. Fans were encouraged to collect all four, which were emblazoned with images of the characters and scenes from Halloween Town and Christmas Town. The watches now sell as collectibles online, going for more money as a four-piece set with the original boxes.

Reflecting back, Burton always hoped there would be memorable toys and collectibles available for *Tim Burton's The Nightmare Before Christmas*, although it took some time for that availability to exist. "When I was growing up I loved toys and being that kind of drawer and designer, I have a big passion for them," Burton notes. "I have toys all over the place." Indeed, as the film began to acquire a bigger fan base, the demand for toys and merchandise grew as well. By the late 1990s, as the film grew in popularity thanks to home video and DVD sales, Disney Parks, Experiences and Products began to respond to the desire for more products. They expanded the original style guide in the late 1990s, offering more opportunities for licensees to incorporate the characters and visual design in toys, dolls, and homeware, and in the late 1990s Disney began selling *Nightmare* items and clothing in Hot Topic stores around the United States.

"I think the demand was always there," says Gentry, who helped create the expanded style guide. "And we were the ones catching up. It seems like we did everything we'd normally do for release, and it was just that the public was asking for more. By the late '90s, that demand was definitely there. That might have actually spurred

Burger King's *Nightmare* watches are now highly collectible.

a bit more interest in the film, because before that you had the film but we didn't quite have all the product people were wanting. So when we put out an assortment it was as if the public couldn't get enough. That spurred on things like the overlay at Disneyland, which created more demand. The opportunity just seems to keep growing."

Today, Burton credits Japanese toy companies with infusing new life into the merchandise created for *Tim Burton's The Nightmare Before Christmas*. Japan was hungry for products after the film came out in theaters there in the fall of

Jack and Sally Dolls

Jack and Sally have the ultimate love story, and over the past few decades brands have released different versions of the beloved couple as dolls—many of which have been packaged together. Popular conceptions of the characters include NECA's marionette dolls, Diamond Select Toys' Jack Skellington and a Sally doll in a double coffin box, and Medicom Toy's dual Bearbrick set, released in 2010. The pair regularly emerges in new variations each year. It's a fun item for fans to collect, but it's also a reminder of the power of the storytelling in *Tim Burton's The Nightmare Before Christmas.*

"Jack and Sally together are number one," McClements says of toy, doll, and product designs. "Them coming together completes both characters—it's such a huge, huge thing. This film is so honest and pure. It's funny to say that about a skeleton and a rag doll, but it really transcends that. It's about the purity of the two characters finding each other. That's something we're all striving for. So when you see those two together they may look like an unlikely pair, but actually it's like, "No, this is exactly who they need.""

Jack and Sally dolls are frequently sold in coffin-shaped boxes.

Over the years, themed *Nightmare* merchandise has become plentiful, from home decor to kitchenware to picnic accessories. (Featured here are a selection of Hot Topic's *Tim Burton's The Nightmare Before Christmas* merchandise, including the tea set, cutting boards, and crockpot. Additional images are courtesy of Disney.)

1994, and Japanese doll company JUN Planning, Inc.—now based in South Korea—created numerous lines of action figures, figurines, and dolls beginning in the late 1990s. Several of the dolls, including limited edition variations on Jack Skellington, arrived in coffin-shaped boxes. A "Gold Millennium Edition," released in the year 2000 with a limited run of 2,000, is one of the most striking: Jack's body, head, and clothing are coated in gold as he resides in a gold coffin. JUN Planning, Inc.'s figures are notably detailed, often including accessories for the characters. In 2004, for the tenth anniversary of the film in Japan, the company designed a set with Lock, Shock, and Barrel riding in their bathtub, as well as a Jack figure who came with an angry face and a chair. "I think it struck a chord in Japan particularly," remembers Heinrichs. "There was a lot of interest and appetite for the merch from their side—and some pretty cool clothing and toys came out of their exploration of our graphic language, as well."

"Disney was known for doing good merchandise, but then this Japanese company came in and shamed all of us into going, 'Wow,'" Burton adds. "They made amazing toys. And then Disney started to do things more in that zone of what the Japanese had created and it was great

stuff. It was exactly what I would have hoped for from the beginning. You could use those as stop-motion puppets, almost. They were fantastic. For me, it revolutionized it."

Action figures based on the movie continued to be extremely popular, particularly as these new designs emerged. In 2002, collectible merchandising company NECA unveiled several Nightmare marionettes, followed by four life-sized plush dolls of Jack and Sally in 2003. In 2004, NECA debuted a new line of action figures with a similar sensibility to the early Hasbro ones. Six lines were released in total from 2004 to 2007, and nearly every character in the film, from Jack to the melting man to Igor, was included. Two exclusives, Vampire Jack and Pirate Jack, were sold at San Diego Comic-Con, and the company also offered several boxed sets of the action figures. One of the boxed sets, notably, was Jack Skellington with multiple heads, evoking the highly sought after "12 Faces of Jack."

Over the past decade, the products and toys available for the beloved film have multiplied exponentially. Disney Parks, Experiences and Products has expanded its offerings to encompass fans of all ages, and there are even items for beloved family pets. The response is always

Left: Funko dolls of Sally, Jack, and Santa; *Right:* A light-up Zero doll.

An original Oogie Boogie puppet sold at auction in 2010.

fan-led, with the company responding to how much interest it sees for toys and merchandise. But as much as the product lines grow, those behind the scenes keep Burton's original film as their inspiration. Gentry aims to bring the movie's aesthetic and tone into each toy he supervises by emphasizing storytelling.

"When you're working on something you say, 'What is the story?'" Gentry explains. "What story are you trying to tell? And sometimes that story is as simple as a single, favorite character that a kid can play with or that an adult can look back at. But we try to infuse as much storytelling into it as we can. An animator has hundreds of drawings or frames to be able to tell a story, but in our case, when we design a toy, we have one drawing to tell the story. And then, of course,

whoever is purchasing can interact with it and continue the story."

One example of that is a series of *Tim Burton's The Nightmare Before Christmas* Hot Wheels cars, first released in 2018 for the twenty-fifth anniversary of the film. The initial eight cars interpreted the characters as existing Hot Wheels vehicles, with Jack Skellington as a Street Creeper, Oogie Boogie as a Super Van, and Sally as a custom 1969 Volkswagen Squareback. After those sold out, the company followed up with another set, this time as character cars that adapted each character's physical attributes into a corresponding custom Hot Wheels. The brand has continued to sell themed cars, and even created a short stop-motion film with the Jack and Sally cars for the holidays in 2021.

Christmas Ornaments and Festive Curiosities

Throughout the years, the world of *Tim Burton's The Nightmare Before Christmas* has brought a sense of festive cheer to fans around Christmas time. Through Christmas tree ornaments, holiday decorations, and even advent calendars, Jack and his crew help to liven up every home.

The film's world and characters often decorate fans' homes during the holiday season as ornaments, miniatures, and stockings. (Images on this page and the advent calendar opposite are from Bradford Exchange. Ornament and stocking images on the opposite page are from Hot Topic's *Tim Burton's The Nightmare Before Christmas* collection.)

Sometimes, the storytelling in products is less about replicating something from the film directly and more about using the characters or the aesthetic as a point of reference. In 2015, artist Jasmine Becket-Griffith designed a collection of fairy figurines inspired by *Tim Burton's The Nightmare Before Christmas*, sold via the Hamilton Collection. Becket-Griffith imagined her signature fairies holding *Nightmare* dolls, including Jack, Sally, Oogie Boogie, and Zero, which were sold with a Halloween Town display. More recently, Hot Topic began selling a Jack Skellington cheese board, a black-and-white *Nightmare* slow cooker, and a wooden serving plank emblazoned with the phase "Now and forever." For the summer of 2021, the designers came up with a collection of beach-themed items, including an Igloo cooler, which were promoted at an event in New York dubbed the "Halloween Town Beach Club."

"It's very visually arresting and it's unexpected for summer, so you get an instant smile on your face," explains Barkan. "People get a kick out of it because it's very unexpected. It lets you not only express your love for something like this, but it also lets you—in the way that you're comfortable—be disruptive."

Tim Burton's The Nightmare Before Christmas continues to be reimagined in creative, compelling ways, often from unexpected brands or retailers. Jack and Sally were crafted into a LEGO Brick Headz set for the film's twenty-fifth anniversary, and in 2019, the characters appeared in LEGO's Disney Series 2 minifigures set alongside Minnie and Mickey, Elsa and Anna, and Jasmine and Jafar. Funko has reimagined the inhabitants of Halloween Town in a variety of ways, including in an advent calendar and as glow-in-the-dark figures. For Burton, the best toys and collectibles capture the essence of *Nightmare* without compromising his early sketches of the character.

"Because the toys come in different forms, not all of them actually fit with the initial design of the character," Burton reflects. "But when a brand gets it right, they get the spirit of the character and that's what I like. You can remain true to the character, but do it in a slightly different style. With Funko, it's a big head and short fat body—well, that's not Jack, but if you do it the right way it's got a charm and it fits both the toy and the spirit of the character."

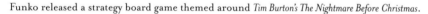

Funko released a strategy board game themed around *Tim Burton's The Nightmare Before Christmas*.

©Disney

VIDEO GAMES AND BOARD GAMES

Although *Tim Burton's The Nightmare Before Christmas* is full of memorable visuals and exciting adventures, it took some time for games to be developed based on the original world of the film. Over the past few decades, more and more board games themed to the movie have appeared in stores, but the first time characters from *Nightmare* appeared in a video game wasn't until 2002, with the release of *Kingdom Hearts*.

The action role-playing game featured a protagonist named Sora who teamed up with Disney characters like Goofy and Donald Duck to fight a group of villains called the Heartless. Gameplay included a visit to Halloween Town, where Jack and the Evil Scientist attempt to help stop the Heartless, but are foiled by Oogie Boogie. The battle then makes its way to Christmas Town, as well, and other *Nightmare* characters, including Sally and Zero, pop up as the story unfolds. Since then, Jack Skellington and his pals have continued to appear in the *Kingdom Hearts* series. The Pumpkin King, along with the Evil Scientist,

Top: Jack in *Disney Mirrorverse*; *Middle: Disney Emoji Blitz*; *Bottom: Fall Guys: Ultimate Knockout.*

showed up in 2004's *Kingdom Hearts: Chain of Memories* and played a key role in *Kingdom Hearts II*, released in the US in 2005. Jack was also a part of 2009's *Kingdom Hearts 358/2 Days*.

Meanwhile, thanks to the immense popularity of the film in Japan, game company Capcom began developing a stand-alone video game that would act as a sequel to the film. The design team created an action-adventure video game for PlayStation 2, GameCube, and Xbox titled *Tim Burton's The Nightmare Before Christmas: Oogie's Revenge*, which was released in Japan in 2004 and in the United States in 2005. It follows the events of the film, with Lock, Shock, and Barrel resurrecting Oogie Boogie when Jack leaves town to seek out new ideas for Halloween. Upon Jack's return, the day before Christmas Eve, the Pumpkin King discovers he needs to save Halloween Town—and Sally—from Oogie Boogie yet again. The game was created with the

approval of Burton, as well as design consultation from *Nightmare*'s art director Deane Taylor.

"They said, 'We've been looking for someone who can give the team an insight into the heart of the film,'" Taylor recalls. "They said, 'Because the game that they're producing, they're producing it beautifully, but it's a copy. We want to find out where Jack Skellington's heart is.' So, how could they build that into the personality of the game?"

Bottom: Jack joins the quest in *Kingdom Hearts*.
Right: Lock, Shock, and Barrel in *Disney Magic Kingdoms*.

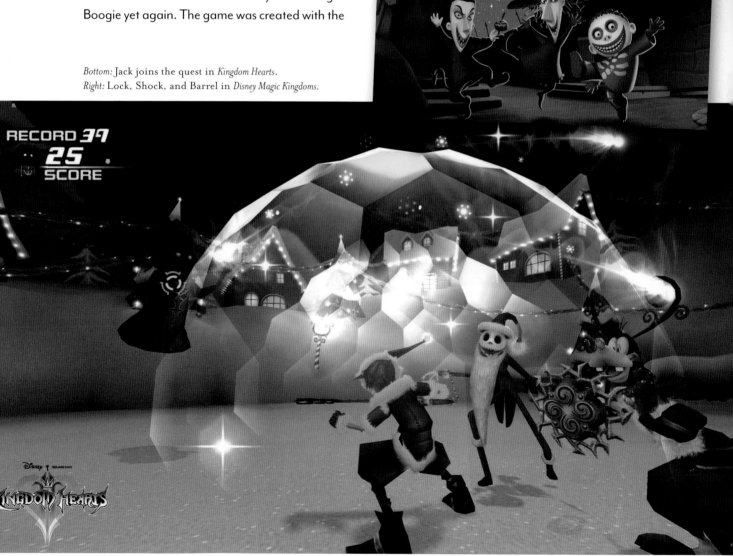

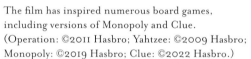

The film has inspired numerous board games, including versions of Monopoly and Clue. (Operation: ©2011 Hasbro; Yahtzee: ©2009 Hasbro; Monopoly: ©2019 Hasbro; Clue: ©2022 Hasbro.)

The following year, Game Boy Advance unveiled *Tim Burton's The Nightmare Before Christmas: The Pumpkin King*, a prequel to the film. Also originally developed in Japan, by Tose, the platform game centered on Jack Skellington's first encounter with Oogie Boogie, who desires to turn Halloween into Crawloween. The action sees Jack rescuing Sally for the first time, resulting in their initial meeting, and he defeats Oogie Boogie, who declares he will get his revenge.

Since then, the characters of *Tim Burton's The Nightmare Before Christmas* have populated multi-IP games like *Disney Infinity*, *Disney Magical World*, *Disney Magic Kingdoms*, *Disney Emoji Blitz*, and *Disney Sorcerer's Arena*. Alongside characters from *Pirates of the Caribbean* and *Tron*, they are among the Disney characters that video game developers ask for most.

"*The Nightmare Before Christmas* really resonates with the gaming audience," explains Sonoko Ishioka, Executive Producer for Walt Disney Games. "The characters fit really well in different contexts. We can do something playful and funny, or we can do something more serious and action-oriented. The characters are versatile with great fantastical traits. It's not about them just existing in a multi-IP universe of the game. We always think about, 'What is the version of Jack that appears in this world with all these characters?' We think about what his essence is, what his traits are, and then translate that in terms of both gameplay and art style."

In December of 2021, popular video game *Fall Guys: Ultimate Knockout* launched a limited-edition collection of *Tim Burton's The Nightmare Before Christmas* character costumes. Players could use their "Kudos" points to acquire The Mayor of Halloween Town, Sally, and Jack Skellington, and to play event challenges featuring Santa Jack and Zero. The event was an example of a collaboration that helped to introduce the film to the audience in a new way.

"It was a very successful event that was well-received," Ishioka says. "It generated really great user engagement, both in the game and on social media. The players of *Fall Guys* are young people, so they may not have seen *The Nightmare Before Christmas*. Maybe they're being introduced and they're like, 'Well, this is cool. What is that?' And then they go check out the movie, they become fans, and we get to tell even more stories. That's a really exciting thing about being able to work with the film in the games."

Jack and Oogie Boogie also joined the fun in *Disney Mirrorverse*, a mobile action RPG game released in June of 2022. In the game, alternate-reality versions of the characters can team up with more than forty other alternate-reality versions of Disney heroes and villains to protect the Mirrorverse from the threat of an enemy called The Fractured.

For players who prefer a more tactile experience, board games continue to be a hit with fans of the film. Themed versions of games like Yahtzee—which uses Jack's head to shake the dice—have been particularly popular over the past decade. One of the first board games, released by NECA in 2004, was an original game titled *Tim Burton's The Nightmare Before Christmas* Board Game. Players were tasked with kidnapping Sandy Claws and defeating Oogie Boogie—much like the film itself. Now a collectible, the game featured six metal game pieces: Jack, Sally, the Evil Scientist, and Lock, Shock, and Barrel.

Later, a chess set, released for the twenty-fifth anniversary, featured Jack as the king of the white game pieces and Oogie Boogie as the king of the black game pieces. Oogie Boogie is also the subject of a themed edition of Operation, where players are tasked with removing items from the villain's body without setting off the buzzer. There are also *Tim Burton's The Nightmare Before Christmas* versions of Monopoly, Clue, Something Wild!, Trivial Pursuit, Jenga, and Scrabble, as well as puzzles, playing cards, and dice, which come emblazoned with the characters' faces. For many, actively participating in a game allows fans to immerse themselves in the film's story and continue to keep it alive.

FASHION AND STYLE

For a fan of *Tim Burton's The Nightmare Before Christmas*, a Jack Skellington T-shirt is the ultimate fashion statement. But it's not the only sartorial way fans can express their love of the film. In fact, *Nightmare*-themed fashion dates back to before the movie's arrival. In October of 1993, as *Tim Burton's The Nightmare Before Christmas* was arriving in theaters, Macy's department store in New York City installed temporary window displays themed to the film. The displays featured small sets from the movie inhabited by characters like Oogie Boogie and props like a headless doll.

But despite the spotlight on the film in a major shopping destination, early apparel options were limited—as with the toys and merchandise. For the most part, *Nightmare* clothing items sold in 1993 were T-shirts featuring Jack Skellington. There was a memorable "Bone Daddy" T-shirt, featuring Jack posing in front of a sepia-toned background, as well as several shirts with artwork and lettering from the film, including one depicting Jack on Spiral Hill. However, some of what is sold online

and in secondhand shops today as "vintage" *Nightmare* apparel may have been fan-made due to the lack of variation in stores.

As with the toys, the fashion options have grown significantly. A major player in that growth has been retailer Hot Topic, which has hundreds of stores throughout the US, as well as a strong online presence. Orv and LeAnn Madden started Hot Topic out of their Southern California garage in October of 1989 and the store became integral to American malls, particularly in the 1990s and 2000s. It continues to be an essential stop in any teenage shopping experience—although some of that experience has now shifted online.

Everything in a Hot Topic store is slightly off-kilter and there's a sense of shared community and fan identity among those who frequent the shops. Early on, Hot Topic sold *Nightmare* T-shirts, Jack Skellington beanies, and accessories alongside toys and collectibles. A favorite item, which continues to be re-released in a new form each year, was the Bone Daddy cologne and Rag Doll perfume. The first year Hot Topic sold *Nightmare* merchandise the sales numbers were ten times

Jack and Sally feature on jewelry created to promote the film. (Pictured here are pieces from RockLove Jewelry's *Tim Burton's The Nightmare Before Christmas* collection.)

Fans can celebrate their love of *Nightmare* with makeup sets. (Pictured here is part of Colourpop Cosmetics' Tim Burton's *The Nightmare Before Christmas* makeup collection.)

what was projected. "It was highly successful for Hot Topic," confirms Senior Vice President General Merchandise Manager Ed La Bay, who oversees the buyers and marketing for the retailer.

By the 2000s, Hot Topic was selling enormous amounts of product tied to *Tim Burton's The Nightmare Before Christmas*. The available items began to increase both in number and in creativity, with additions like homeware, car accessories, and beauty products. In the early years there were less than twenty *Nightmare*-themed items sold in Hot Topic; today, there are more than four hundred. The interest from consumers has evolved as the film has embedded itself more fully in pop culture. Jack and Sally remain very popular, but more and more merchandise is inspired by Oogie Boogie, including makeup palettes. *Nightmare* is consistently in the top ten franchises sold at Hot Topic among Harry Potter, Star Wars, and Marvel, particularly during the fall and holiday seasons. "Even with changing trends *Nightmare* will still find its voice and be a major property for us in the back half of the year," La Bay says. "Regardless of

the trend cycle between genres and pop culture, *Nightmare* always has a home."

As the film remains perpetually popular, Hot Topic does adapt its themed apparel to contemporary fashion trends. Sally dresses, in particular, are redesigned each year to reflect what consumers, especially in the Hot Topic demographic of late teens and early twenties, are wearing. The Sally replica dress is updated annually, adapting the silhouette or the hemline to embrace current customer tastes. Similarly, swimsuits, like a two-piece Jack suit replica, have become a sought-after look. Because *Tim Burton's The Nightmare Before Christmas* merchandise and apparel now saturates the marketplace, Hot Topic aims to keep pushing the envelope while staying true to Burton's vision.

"One reason why *Nightmare* is able to continue to find its voice every year is that it's so transcendent and so easily applied to trend categories," La Bay explains. "Whether it's an iconic Jack head image, which in the beginning was what drove the product line, to around ten years ago starting to see that Sally cosplay really take shape. We always want to be a destination

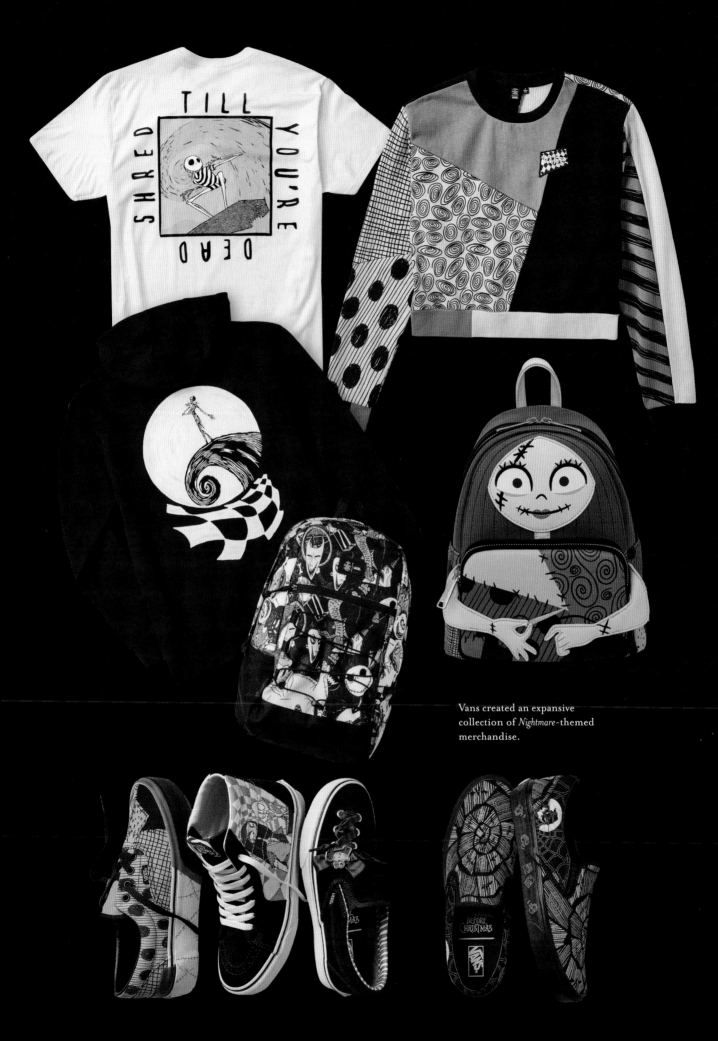

Vans created an expansive collection of *Nightmare*-themed merchandise.

Special edition adidas Crazy 8 sneakers, released in 2013.

for the next cool item. We want to keep it fresh for the fan. And a bit of scarcity with the product never hurts—we want there to be a chase factor. So if you are lucky enough to get the product this year, that feels special and unique."

Outside of Hot Topic, over the past decade, fashion collaborations have become increasingly popular with fans of *Tim Burton's The Nightmare Before Christmas*, with more brands jumping onboard. For the holidays in 2013, adidas released a special edition of Kobe Bryant's retro Crazy 8 silhouette basketball shoe. In October of 2019, Vans unveiled a special collection inspired by *Nightmare*, which featured ten pieces of footwear along with various apparel and accessory items. The highlight of the collection was a pair of Sk8-Hi shoes depicting "Jack's Lament," with four panels showcasing frames from Jack's walk through the Halloween Town cemetery. Oogie Boogie, Sally, and Lock, Shock, and Barrel were also spotlighted on various styles, from high-top sneakers to slip-ons. But rather than simply inserting artwork from the film directly onto the shoes, the designers aimed to make something more creative that engaged fans in a more nuanced, clever way.

"It was really cool and it really spoke to the storytelling of the film," Javier Garcia, senior manager of product design at Disney Parks, Experiences and Products, explains of the collection. "Those details speak really loudly to the fan and really engage that fan. *The Nightmare*

Before Christmas fan is one of those 'If you know, you know' Disney fans where they love to latch on to key details that maybe you don't catch the first time you watch the film."

A streetwear or skate brand like Vans is the perfect fit for *Tim Burton's The Nightmare Before Christmas*, but Disney also looks to more unexpected brands like MeUndies, which sells *Nightmare*-themed pajamas, boxers, bras, and underwear. The initial collection in 2021 was so desirable that it sold out almost immediately. According to Garcia, the undergarment line is one of the most successful *Nightmare* collaborations to date. Also successful: apparel for children, infants, and pets. While the primary age range for *Nightmare* fashion is eighteen to thirty-five, Disney introduced kids' products in the late 2010s and added on an infant selection in the early 2020s. "There was so much demand in those categories that we opened it up because the fan was really adamant about getting this for their kids," Garcia says. "Now, it's a full family statement."

Jack Skellington T-shirts remain a staple, but Disney Parks, Experiences and Products also endeavors to design apparel options that hint at the visual aesthetic and themes of the film without looking like a replica or a costume. Nuanced detailing is used to evoke the film so only those in the know will notice its connection.

"We on the apparel side wouldn't necessarily approve a dress for someone like Hot Topic that

is an exact replica—it has to be inspired by the characters," Garcia explains. "We look more at what fashion silhouettes there are. Like a skater jersey dress for women that is inspired by Sally's dress, but it isn't necessarily exactly like Sally's dress. I want it to stay true to the story and I want it to speak directly to the fan. We have these winks and nods. These little hidden details. Whether it's pocket lining patterns, little color trims that tie back to the character, or even thread colors that complement what a character's costume is like. So black denim with white stitching like Jack's suit. I just love to convey the personality of the characters and the story."

Outside of the official apparel designs, Disney fans have found ways to draw the imagery from the film into their day-to-day looks. The most notable trend is DisneyBounding, a way of evoking a character's look without a costume or a direct replica of their outfit. DisneyBound, or "bounding," involves creating an outfit inspired by a favorite character in a casual, creative way. The idea is to take advantage of whatever is already in one's closet, using color blocking, a pattern, or a specific silhouette to hint at Jack or Sally. It's a trend that's become especially popular in the Disney Parks, but, of course, fans can bound anywhere, any time.

Child and infant apparel has become increasingly popular for fans of the film. (Featured here, clockwise from top, are pants from Rags, shoes from Freshly Picked, a sweatshirt from Little Sleepies, and a pajama shirt from Hanna Anderson.)

Left: Leslie Kay and pals Disney bound characters from the film; *Right:* A *Nightmare*-inspired outfit by Margo Donis.

"I find Disney bounders gravitate towards *The Nightmare Before Christmas*," says Leslie Kay, who began chronicling Disney-inspired fashion on her blog over a decade ago. "I think for a lot of us we went through our punk phase—or maybe it wasn't even a phase—when we were in high school. That was around when *The Nightmare Before Christmas* had its second resurgence and it became more than just a movie. It became a cultural phenomenon, really. And it's such a wearable movie because it has the pinstripes and haunting silhouettes and patchwork. It's all very accessible within mass fashion."

Although Disney-themed bounding is a trend year-round, many bounders have traditionally embraced the film's characters beginning in September and extending through the fall. Now, with the addition of Halfway to Halloween as an annual celebration, *Nightmare* becomes fashion throughout the entire year. For many, it's a way to explore the Disney Parks, particularly the *Haunted Mansion* overlay, as a character without an actual costume.

"There's a reason why most of the bounders are so obsessed with Halloween," Kay says. "We want to live that day year-round and when you're Disney bounding it allows you to do it in

a way where you're playing dress up and you are embodying this character, but it's more for you than it is for the shock factor of an amazing costume. If you're bounding as Jack you don't necessarily have to suddenly start acting like Jack. But I do find that if I'm doing it at a park, I start to explore the park as if I am Jack Skellington or Sally, because you want to go to places that they would go. I find it does guide your day differently."

Tim Burton's The Nightmare Before Christmas inspires many fans, but not all interpret the visual aesthetic of the film so literally. Fan Margo Donis incorporates the Gothic world of *Nightmare* into her everyday looks without necessarily trying to mimic anything directly.

"I think the idea of adding holidays, especially Halloween, into fashion makes it fun and a bit of a challenge, especially when things come out once a year," Donis says. "But that's why it's fun to find colors and looks that fit the genre. I love to look for colors that match specific characters if I'm going for a specific look. My favorite character's aesthetic is Jack Skellington, simple and easy. The movie is so different from any Disney movie out there and I connect with the characters in a lot of ways, so it's exciting to bring them into my wardrobe."

Halloween Costumes

Today, trick-or-treaters regularly don Halloween costumes inspired by the characters and the story of *Tim Burton's The Nightmare Before Christmas*. But before *Nightmare* was a complete film, artistic coordinator Allison Abbate created the first-ever Sally Halloween costume. The movie's crew, comprised of artistic, creative people, held Halloween parties where everyone dressed up in a costume of their own making. For the event, Abbate drew stitches across her face and donned a costume that evoked Sally's final look in the film.

"I saw a sketch for the sculpt, so I used dresses that I had and then crafted them together into the shape," Abbate remembers. "We hadn't created the puppet yet so no one knew the character and I don't even know if Sally had a costume yet. I didn't have the right patterns or fabric, so I did my own interpretation. It was definitely a very DIY costume. But one of the great things about working in stop-motion is that everyone's so talented, and so our Halloween parties were truly the stuff of legend. The creativity and craftsmanship the artists showcased was amazing. People would go all out, so I always felt like I needed to really do it up right to compete."

Abbate may have been the first to dress up as a character from the film, but she has certainly not been the last. From Sally to Oogie Boogie to Jack to Shock, adults and children alike have donned Halloween costumes inspired by the film. Some fans prefer to create their own, often crafting their own take on a favorite character, while others shop Disney's official line of *Nightmare* Halloween costumes. There are Jack masks, Sally wigs, and Zero ensembles for family pups. Over the years, as *Tim Burton's The Nightmare Before Christmas* has become a Halloween tradition, the film has spawned thousands upon thousands of Halloween costumes, each with its own unique nod to Burton's original vision.

Nightmare Halloween costumes have been popular since even before the film was released.

5

KEEPING THE MAGIC ALIVE

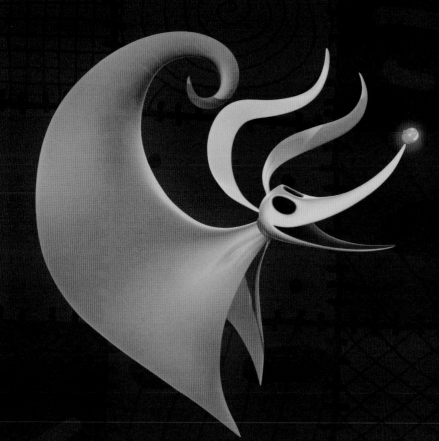

FANDOM, COSPLAY, AND WEDDINGS

Although *Tim Burton's The Nightmare Before Christmas* owes a significant amount of its ongoing success to its visual and thematic artistry, the film is also indebted to its fans. What started as a cult classic transformed into a mainstream pop culture phenomenon that is embraced by viewers in all walks of life. It's clear that without its devoted audience *Nightmare* wouldn't have been so pervasive. But, of course, the film's relationship with its fanbase isn't one-sided. It's a symbiotic bond that creates an ongoing sense of connection and creativity on both sides. As *Nightmare* has taken on a life of its own, it has also become the inspiration for many things that exist outside of it, from weddings to cosplay to full-sleeve tattoos. In that way, the film lives on because of the fans and they carry on because of it.

Early on, the fans of the film were linked to specific subcultures: devotees of Tim Burton, Goth kids, classic horror fans, and lovers of Halloween. At the time, there was no social media to fuel the fire. Instead, fans shared their love through word of mouth or by wearing a favorite Jack Skellington T-shirt. Because it wasn't yet possible to congregate on the Internet, the movie saw a slow burn in fan circles around the world, particularly in the United States, United Kingdom, Japan, and Australia. Later, in the 2000s, it was embraced by the emo and hard rock scenes, and became a focal point for teenagers who had grown up watching it. Additionally, as the movie started to become a staple at Disneyland and other Disney Parks each Halloween, audiences began to incorporate it into their annual holiday traditions. As the years went on, the characters popped up in more and more seemingly unexpected places, establishing themselves as cornerstones of pop culture. Instead of captivating varied niche audiences, as it did on its theatrical release, the film has become a beloved, well-known franchise that crosses the mainstream.

"There are people who are fans of the film itself, for the love of what it is as a narrative universe, much like the way that people love *Star Wars* or *Game of Thrones*," explains Dr. James Rendell, a lecturer and researcher who studies onscreen media audiences and identity. "It's so rich that people just love it. But it's also been adopted and celebrated by other aspects of popular culture. When I was growing up, there were loads of cool punk bands that had *Nightmare Before Christmas* tattoos. Blink-182 had the song 'I Miss You' that includes lyrics about Jack and Sally. There are intertextual references, so it has bled into popular culture, perhaps more than people really appreciate. What the film does so well is draw on a lot of different things from horror history and popular culture that fans enjoy, and I think that's reflective of Burton as a director where a lot of his creations are love letters to the things that he adores."

Cosplay has become an important part of *Nightmare* fandom over the years.

Over the years, the filmmakers have been aware of the constant growth of the film's fanbase, which now encompasses several generations. The relationship one has with *Tim Burton's The Nightmare Before Christmas* shifts based on when and how one first experienced it.

"For older people who saw it as kids, it's like a primal memory," says Henry Selick. "Their eyes go wide when they remember that time. Some of them are now old enough that they have kids and they've shown it to them. And then there are younger people who maybe didn't see it initially, but they knew about it. In some cases, they knew about the merchandise first and wanted to know what it meant. But everyone found their way in and it was like a club they wanted to be part of."

While the entry point into the world of *Tim Burton's The Nightmare Before Christmas* may differ from person to person, there are certain things that connect every fan. Like Jack and Sally, everyone has had the feeling of being on the outside, or of being a misfit or an outcast. Everyone can find relatability in the idea of searching for purpose and ultimately finding it within your own community. It's a commonality that features in all of Burton's work, but particularly in *Nightmare*. "Everyone seems grateful to him, particularly young people," Helena Bonham Carter once noted of the filmmaker. "He understands everyone's separateness and isolation, that feeling that you don't fit in or that you're different."

Many of the cast members and filmmakers have visited fan conventions and special screenings of the film regularly over the years. They've seen how the love for the movie has spread and generated its own special community of people. For Chris Sarandon, who continues to do autograph signings and panels at events like Comic Con, it's a testament to how much the film has impacted people's lives.

"When fans see you they want you to understand how profound their experience with the movie has been," Sarandon says. "How it has either entertained them or given them a respite from some difficulty. It's not in a narcissistic way—it's 'I want you to know that you have been important in my life.' In that sense, it's not about me; it's about the movie and it's about the experience. So I do my best to make sure that they know they are seen. It's that human connection. I want to understand why the movie is important to them. It's deeply humbling."

Fans frequently share genuinely personal and moving stories with the cast and filmmakers. While some viewers may simply enjoy the story and the songs, others have found real solace and comfort in the world of Halloween Town. Sarandon and Ken Page both recall encounters with emotional fans who have shared moments of grief and loss. For those fans, *Nightmare* has been a beacon of light in the darkness. "I can't tell you how many young people have come up to me and have said, 'This movie saved my life,'" Sarandon noted. "And very often they're kids who are outsiders."

For a fan of *Tim Burton's The Nightmare Before Christmas*, there are a lot of ways to express a love of the film. People often pull inspiration from Burton's visual aesthetic to create their own unique reflection of the movie and its story, whether it's in the form of a colorful tattoo, detailed nail art, or a batch of Sally-themed cookies. Cosplayers frequently embody the characters, making them feel real in the world. From fan fiction to memes, *Nightmare* is continuously renewed by those who cherish it. For a scrappy stop-motion film that disappeared from the zeitgeist upon its theatrical release, it's an impressive feat—and it's something that Burton takes very seriously.

"It's great and it rarely happens," Burton reflects of the film's fandom. "The idea of a film where that happened feels very special to me because I feel a connection myself. I felt that way and I still feel that way and it is nice to have that connection. I never expected it and it's something that still surprises me. It's crazy and incredible."

EXPRESSIONS OF FANDOM

Tim Burton's The Nightmare Before Christmas is ultimately a visual artistic work. Because of that the movie lends itself well to creative expression that is also visual, whether it's fan art interpretations of the characters or baked goods inspired by the look of Halloween Town. The advent of the Internet and social media has encouraged the sharing of these creations, adding to the inescapable nature of the film in popular culture. Entire blogs are devoted to *Nightmare*-themed recipes and fans share crafts and artwork in Facebook groups and via Instagram and Pinterest.

"A lot of it has to do with the fact that this is a rich tapestry of characters and the story

world is so developed," Rendell says. "What you get with something like *The Nightmare Before Christmas* that's so wonderful and encouraging fans to engage with is that you have a really lovely blend of characters who are fully fleshed out—Jack Skellington, Sally—and we know their trials and tribulations and what makes them tick. And then you also have a whole bunch of secondary characters that you see just for moments, like the witches or the werewolf. Characters who are visually very appealing, but there's scope for them to have more focus or deeper characterization than they are given in the original film. That's where fans can write their own comics, write their own fanfiction, develop these characters, or take things from the story world and put their own stamp on it. It's a big sandbox for fans to play in and to expand in their own original ways."

In particular, the fans of *Tim Burton's The Nightmare Before Christmas* tend to make actual things, from crafts to food to cosplay ensembles. The tangible, three-dimensional sensibility of the film translates well into the real world, which drives a specific type of fan engagement. "The tactile aesthetic of *The Nightmare Before Christmas* with the stop-motion gives a 3D dynamic that lends itself to crafting and creating," Rendell notes. "It also has a distinct visual tone. You don't have to go study art to be able to draw like Tim Burton because he has a childlike quality to his work. That lends itself to people of all ages bringing a Burton-esque style into their creation."

Food, in particular, has become an important way for fans of the movie to relive their favorite moments or to offer their own spin

A handmade version of Jack's house.

Fan-created food and drinks bring the magic of the film into the real world.

on the story. The practice, known to academics as "food craft," has been aided by the official cookbooks and the whimsical, themed dishes and drinks available in the Disney Parks. Although food, birthday cakes, and cocktails are ephemeral and usually quickly consumed, as fans post their creations on social media it becomes a more permanent expression. Popular dishes include iterations of Sally's soup, which she makes in the film, and desserts based on the characters, like a marshmallow Zero or cookies emblazoned with Jack's visage. Not everything is quite so obvious, which allows fans to channel the creativity of the film in their own way.

"There's a real freedom for this stuff, which I think is another reason why fans love the *Nightmare* universe," Rendell notes. "It's not just fans reading comics or playing the video games,

which extend the narrative, but there's a tactile quality to making the craft that allows them to feel close to the film in a different way."

Ginny Phillips, who runs the Disney crafting blog "Making Main Street," has used *Tim Burton's The Nightmare Before Christmas* for inspiration several times because of the way the colors and the simplicity of the aesthetic can be translated into food and home décor. For Halloween 2021, the official Disney Parks Blog tapped Philips to create a treat board that paid homage to Burton's film. Her detailed board featured Sally sugar cookies, Oogie Boogie white chocolate-dipped strawberries, and macarons decorated with Spiral Hill.

"It's so easy to mimic the whole vibe of the movie," Philips explains. "You can simplify it, or you can just make it super detailed with all those textures that are in the movie. It's a very easy world to pull from

Left: Nail art of the characters; *Right:* Fall Out Boy's Pete Wentz shows off his *Nightmare* tattoos.

and to create things from. It's a treasure trove of colors and textures and it's just iconic."

Along with culinary efforts, fans often incorporate the world of the film into their daily lives in inventive ways. Nail art is trendy among fans, who showcase their designs on social media, and some decorate their homes in tribute to the movie on a year-round basis rather than just for the holidays. Even celebrities like Gwen Stefani and Channing Tatum have reimagined the characters for Halloween. One of the most intimate forms of fan expression, however, is tattoos, which are notably prevalent among those who have been personally impacted by the film.

"You can't enter that world yourself because it's animation, but you can make it real in other ways," explains Dr. Rebecca Williams, who researches fandom and fan practices. "I'm always really impressed by the really beautiful artwork that people put on themselves from the film. I've seen quite a lot of people with mash-ups of the film and characters from other Burton films because there's overlap in that iconography. There's a really nice creativity about around it and people play with that."

Selick, who has noticed crossover tattoos that incorporate both *Tim Burton's The Nightmare Before Christmas* and *Coraline*, feels that this permanent

body art reflects the true dedication of the film's fanbase. "What the film has inspired and how the fans have reacted is that some go whole hog," he notes. "It's part of their life so they make it part of their bodies."

Because tattoos are unique to the individual, they're a way to incorporate the film into one's appearance without simply mimicking what already exists. Many fans ask for customized tattoos that incorporate personal elements or that showcase a clever spin on the visual aesthetic of the film. The film's sensibility works as body art because it can be adapted in so many different ways. The actors from the film are also frequently asked to sign fans' tattoos, which they always do with gratitude. O'Hara considers that her favorite piece of merchandise from over the years. "I have signed some beautiful tattoos of Jack and Sally on legs and backs and arms," she remembers.

Ultimately, those who love *Tim Burton's The Nightmare Before Christmas* relate to the film's creative spirit and visual world, and want to bring those elements to life in a more tangible way, whatever that is. By making their favorite characters or scenes concrete, fans can re-live the movie over and over again, always discovering new aspects of its charm and artistry.

COSPLAY

Cosplay, a Japanese term that means "costumed play," is widespread within the fan community of *Tim Burton's The Nightmare Before Christmas*. The practice has been around since well before the film's release, but has grown in popularity in recent decades thanks to social media and fan conventions. The term refers to the act of dressing up as a fictional character from a movie, TV show, book, or video game, but the practice isn't simply about donning a costume—to devoted cosplayers, it goes far beyond that. For many, it can be about embodying someone else, as well as replicating their appearance with clothes, wigs, and makeup. It's as much an emotional and mental experience as a physical one.

Right: Ashley Eckstein debuts a dress designed by Andrew MacLaine, which is made of 500 Jack Skellington Funko heads, in a photo by Mark Edwards; *Below:* A cosplayer dressed as "Lady Skellington" poses during New York Comic Con 2021.

Many of the film's characters, including Jack, Sally, Oogie Boogie, and Lock, Shock, and Barrel, lend themselves well to cosplay by fans of all ages, genders, and backgrounds. Again, it's about bringing the universe of the movie into daily life. "For a lot of people, cosplay is about making something real in the world that isn't tangible," explains Williams. "For Disney cosplayers, in general, it's about bringing animation into the real world through your body. It's also about embodying characters who you like or who you relate to. For people who feel a close connection with those characters, dressing or cosplaying as those characters can allow you to make them your own."

For some fans, cosplay is an opportunity to pay homage to a character. Harli Hanson, of Dragon Ace Cosplay, creates humanized versions of Jack and Oogie Boogie. "The *Nightmare* characters appeal to my love for all things Halloween," Hanson explains. "The film has always held a special place in my heart as a movie I watched as a kid that shaped me into the Halloween-loving person I am today. I've always loved characters like Jack for being loving to everyone around him and Oogie for

wanting to help his family and community out, even if he didn't do it in the best way. I cosplay Oogie because I love cosplaying villains—they're so fun to be able to embody and play around in."

Because cosplay differs from a Halloween costume, many fans have cleverly designed ensembles that represent a creative take on their favorite character rather than an exact replica. There are glamorous Oogie Boogies, gender-bending Jack Skellingtons, and even battle-ready warrior Sallys. TJ Neece cosplays as "Dapper Oogie Boogie," a version of the villain who wears a burlap suit that Neece made himself.

"Having never worked with burlap before, I did a lot of research and sought advice from my other sew-ist friends," he says. "I think what makes it unique is the fact that I've never seen Oogie Boogie cosplayed in a suit format. I even made a lined burlap face mask with some attached insects to wear on the convention floor. When I cosplay it is normally a love letter to the source material. I grew up loving *The Nightmare Before Christmas* and watch it every year. Wearing this cosplay makes me feel even more connected to other fans in the community."

Themed cosplay can be a full family affair.

Top (left): Sylvia Ward; *Top (right):* Cassandra Franklin; *Bottom:* Renske Theuws.

Embodying Sally

On the surface, Sally seems like a simple rag doll. But as the story unfolds it becomes clear that she is far more complex and has far more agency than one might initially assume. Her stitched-together dress and body, accented by her vivid red hair, makes her a perfect character to cosplay. She is popular with adults and children alike, and fans tend to craft either exact replicas of the onscreen version or create something wholly original. Whether it's at D23 Expo, Disney's fan convention, or Comic Con, there have been hundreds of iterations of Sally over the years.

For Sylvia Ward, who cosplays both Sally and Oogie Boogie, the rag dolls reflects her own personality. "I really liked Sally and have always wanted to cosplay her," Ward explains. "I feel she is very caring and different compared to the other creatures and monsters of Halloween Town. She is also motherly because she took care of Jack while he was deep into his research and I am called 'Cosplay Mother' because I take care of everyone. I purchased her dress and added puff paint detailing to all the printed stitches on the dress."

The filmmakers, who have encountered many cosplay looks at conventions and special events, also emphasize how impressive the many takes on the rag doll have been. "I have to say that in the cosplay world the Sallys have been some of the most amazing costumes that I've seen," Rick Heinrichs notes.

Sally is a popular option for cosplayers around the world.

Cosplay opens the door for re-interpretation of the characters, especially in terms of gender. Cassandra Franklin also cosplays as Oogie Boogie, because she loves his song and his character design. Her version incorporates his look from the film along with other influences. "An artist on Instagram drew a gender-bent Oogie Boogie and my mind ran wild with ideas after I came across it," she says. "Burlap is not an expensive textile, and I was inspired by the jazz elements of Oogie Boogie's song and the challenges of using burlap for a gown-type cosplay."

For Franklin, it was compelling to cosplay as a film character who has a villainous aspect to him. "My cosplay was more on the eerie side, which made plenty of adults and children uncomfortable," she remembers. "That was a new experience for me. My appearance made a child cry when our eyes met at a convention. That made me feel a little bad, but also a small amount of pride."

Renske Theuws also embraces a gender-bending take on a character. She frequently cosplays Jack at various fan events and Comic Cons around the Netherlands, where she lives, and says the act of becoming the film's hero brings her a sense of happiness and excitement.

"Jack is my favorite character from *The Nightmare Before Christmas* and also one of my all-time favorite Disney characters," Theuws explains. "I know he's my dad's favorite Disney character, too, so maybe I was a little influenced back in the day. I really like Jack's outfit and general vibe, but at the same time wanted to make my own version of the character to cosplay. So, it became a female version to stay close to myself, but also to stay close to Jack's design in the movie. I love to wear something that I worked hard on and love to act in a Jack-like way for a day."

Other fans aim for complete adherence to the original film designs. Samantha Giacomini embodies Jack with a replica suit and face paint. "I cosplay Jack Skellington because he is the main character and I love how curious he is

Fans cosplaying *Nightmare* characters at Los Angeles Comic Con.

about everything, especially when he comes to Christmas Town and he wants to know everything about it and he wants to share it with everyone from Halloween Town," she explains. "It was fun to create his iconic face because he has such expressive faces throughout the movie."

There's a strong sense of community spirit among the cosplayers, particularly when they spot someone else cosplaying a character from *Tim Burton's The Nightmare Before Christmas*. That members-only club feeling exists because the film attracts a particular type of cosplayer.

"It is such a drastically different style from all other Disney movies, so it appeals to a completely different crowd," Franklin says. "It doesn't focus on a princess, and although there is a love story between Jack and Sally, I consider that aspect more of a side story. The main story revolves around Jack's adventure to break his usual, boring routine by taking matters into his own hands. The mesh of two vastly different holidays is such a fun concept. *The Nightmare Before Christmas* is an original, creative and visually beautiful film making it a true classic."

ROMANCE AND WEDDINGS

At the end of *Tim Burton's The Nightmare Before Christmas*, Jack and Sally embrace on Spiral Hill, the snow gleaming underneath them. It's a poignant moment to conclude the story, which is about finding a sense of belonging with other misfits. "I wanted something quite simple because he's misguided and she's got her own issues and it felt real to me," Burton recalls of concocting the couple's romance. "He's so single-minded and she's a fragmented character but with equal passion and focus in her own way. It just felt like a real relationship to me."

Because of that authenticity, Jack and Sally's love story has transcended the film and become a focal point for many fans. Couples, no matter their sexuality, relate to the pair's journey to find a soulmate. That has translated into themed Valentine's Day celebrations, engagements, bachelorette and bachelor weekends, anniversaries, and, of course, weddings, all of which take inspiration from Jack and Sally's eventual coupling up in the film. *Nightmare* wedding cakes, which draw on the visual design and the colors in the movie, are particularly widespread. It's all a way to make the onscreen fantasy into reality.

"I think the reasons why *The Nightmare Before Christmas* makes for wonderful inspiration for décor and wedding styling are very much the same as why it's a film everyone loves and watches again and again," explains wedding planner Valentina Ring. "The colors, aesthetic, and details are absolutely iconic and one-of-a-kind, and frame a love story that isn't perfect or typical and is all the more endearing for it. The theme, at the very heart of it, is love that transcends all boundaries of time and space, life and death, and of two souls so entwined that nothing can keep them apart. It's a nostalgic and romantic cult reference, particularly for a certain generation, and one that offers couples a way

Jack and Sally's relationship has influenced many real-life couples.

to express themselves and weave their own style into their celebration."

Ring designed a particularly evocative elopement held in London on the twenty-fifth anniversary of *Tim Burton's The Nightmare Before Christmas*. Working in collaboration with hair and makeup artist Kayleigh Keen, the event, held in a derelict church, imagined the nuptials of Jack and Sally. They wanted to echo Burton's work in the details of the wedding with a dark, moody color palette and a wooden carving of Spiral Hill. Keen's three-legged dog stood in as Zero in a tiny black bow tie.

"Since then, I've had a lot of clients refer to these images and ask for particular details or nods to be incorporated in their wedding design, as a way of personalizing their celebration and adding fun little surprises for their guests to discover," Ring says. "I love that this photoshoot has inspired couples to think outside the box when it comes to their wedding styling, and helped them let go of preconceptions and expectations of what a wedding should look like. Weddings are an opportunity to tell a story, and so should reflect the quirks and histories and values of each individual couple."

One such couple, Julie Shepard and her husband Doug, had been cosplaying Sally and Jack for several years before their wedding, which made it even more poignant when he referenced the film during their vows. "At the end of his vows, he started reciting, 'My dearest friend, if you don't mind, I'd like to join you by your side,'" Shepard

remembers. "And of course I joined him—through my tears—to finish the quote as Sally does in the movie."

For Shepard, channeling the onscreen duo felt relatable. "I think it appeals to couples because Jack and Sally are not a traditional romantic pair," she says. "How often do a skeleton and a living rag doll even get to be shown as more than monsters? And here they are, not only as fully-realized characters with desires and flaws, but also falling in love. It's a nice thought for those of us who feel more raggedy than royal that we get happy endings too."

Kristen Vaughn-Smith and Avery Smith, who married in 2021 at The Old Woolen Mill in Cleveland, Tennessee, took things a step further

A *Nightmare*-themed elopement planned by Valentina Ring.

Kristen Vaughn-Smith and Avery Smith celebrated with a *Nightmare*-inspired wedding. (Photos by Erin Morrison Photography.)

and threw an entire wedding themed around *Tim Burton's The Nightmare Before Christmas*. Every element of the celebration was inspired by the film, from the cake to the invitations to the wedding gown to the décor.

"*The Nightmare Before Christmas* has always been a connecting factor for us," Vaughn-Smith explains. "Avery always knew it was my favorite movie and he gifted me the soundtrack on purple vinyl for the first birthday of mine that we celebrated together. I also got to share the film with Avery for the first time then. We feel that we have a special 'Jack and Sally' connection. We knew we wanted a theme for our wedding

that wasn't too over-the-top or childlike with Halloween decorations. Something that represented us and would be timeless and unforgettable. Something as unique as the film."

The immersive wedding details reflected elements of the film. The ring box, engraved with "Simply meant to be," was coffin-shaped and featured images of Jack and Sally, while a "'Til Death" neon sign illuminated the wedding venue. During the reception, the couple sat in ghost chairs decorated with corresponding "His Sally" and "Her Jack" lettering. The pair walked down the aisle to a song from the film and

played blink-182's "I Miss You" as their wedding party was introduced. While not all of the guests had seen the movie, it created a welcoming vibe that felt perfectly suited to the nuptials.

"Our guests seemed to genuinely enjoy the theme," Vaughn-Smith says. "Many said they were expecting scary due to the old venue's appearance on the outside and the theme, but they instead found the wedding to be beautiful and unlike anything they'd ever seen—in a good way. They also said they wouldn't have expected anything less from us."

For the couple, *Tim Burton's The Nightmare Before Christmas* was a way to tap into their nostalgia for a beloved film while also emphasizing the romantic elements of the story. Since their wedding, they've had other couples reach out looking to do something similar. "I think the love story is so inspiring to people because it's different," Vaughn-Smith reflects. "It demonstrates that no matter how different, weird, or unique you are or how you may not fit in with others, there is a person out there for you and that person actually understands you."

6

REPRISE

AN ONGOING LEGACY

Three decades after its release, it's clear that *Tim Burton's The Nightmare Before Christmas* is still gaining momentum. The film continues to reach new audiences in a variety of ways. Its handmade artistry stands out, both against computer-generated animation and against the general landscape of Hollywood filmmaking. It resonates because it contains something truly special: genuine emotion.

"People like to feel things," explains Brian Volk-Weiss, director of *The Holiday Movies That Made Us*. "It could be happiness, with laughter, or it could be sadness, with crying. It can be shock. It can be horror. But I think ninety-nine percent of movies do not make you feel something. You may be entertained, you may enjoy it, but you don't have an involuntary, visceral reaction to a moment or a song or an event or an action or a line of dialogue. Only one percent of movies make you feel something. That's what makes it connect. Every movie I love or that we've done shows about makes you feel something. This movie makes you feel a lot of things."

Over the years, the film has created its own community. Fans connect over a shared love of the stories, characters, and visual elements. They have formed fan clubs online and via social media. They congregate around holidays in celebration. They show the film to their friends, their families, and their children, passing it along to new viewers, who also become fans. If someone feels isolated or alone, it can be a comforting reminder that everyone is in this together.

"There's something in its fundamental Tim Burton-ness, that story of loneliness, that really communicates with people," film historian Ian Nathan says. "It's quite traditional, although

Jack Skellington ultimately finds his purpose in Halloween Town.

it's not a traditional way of telling it—the idea of someone who doesn't belong somewhere or who thinks they don't belong somewhere is a classic movie setup. To my mind, it's Burton's best animated film, even though he didn't direct it. It's an extension of his sketches. It's an extension of the way he draws more than any other film. So you have that lovely peculiar-ness to it, which gives you really great images. In its heart—and it literally has a big heart—it's a film about weirdos. And everybody in the world, on some level, thinks they're a weirdo. Jack speaks to them. Tim speaks to them. That's very resonant for people."

Those who created the film look back on the experience with pride. It was a singular moment in many of their careers and the filmmakers don't take that fact lightly. For Selick, it represents a clarity of vision and expression that is unmatched by the typical Hollywood production process.

"A huge amount of creativity and love went into the movie," Henry Selick says. "I think it's so rare for that to happen, especially since it took several years to make the film. You can see indie features out there done quickly on a low budget that have a complete artistic vision. But it's rare for something like this. I feel it's very pure and represents everyone's best intentions."

The many faces of Jack Skellington.

"Aside from the great story and songs, it looks amazing," Catherine O'Hara adds. "The character designs, the sets, the spectacular creativity that went into executing the stop-motion animation. I got to see the artists making the movie in San Francisco and I wish everyone could see that in person. They created every moment in the movie literally by hand, manipulating the set pieces and props and miraculously bringing the characters to life."

Burton has embraced the film as dearly as its fans. What began as an idea in his head now exists as a cultural phenomenon that connects people around the world. It was a long journey to arrive at *Tim Burton's The Nightmare Before Christmas*, but the fact that it was made at all remains a point of pride. Everyone who has touched *Nightmare* and everyone who has been touched by it now share in its success.

"It just felt like a special moment because there wasn't a lot of this kind of stuff going on," Burton says. "It felt different at the time. All the amazing artists that did it and made it, all the stuff to get it made, the time it took, and all of that, and then I finally saw it through. That's why it remains one of the most special projects, because of all the elements that went into it."

Jack Skellington finds himself during a journey of ups and downs.

ACKNOWLEDGMENTS

Writing a book can feel like a solitary effort, but this book, like *Tim Burton's The Nightmare Before Christmas*, was brought together—and made better—by an amazing crew of people.

First and foremost, thank you to Delia Greve, who conceived the idea of a book exploring the cultural legacy of Tim Burton's amazing film and brought me on board. Thank you to my supportive editors Katie Moore and Katie McGuire, my intrepid photo researcher Julie Alissi, and my publisher Rage Kindelsperger. Thank you to Laura Drew and Kim Winscher, who created the layout for this book. Thank you to Steve Roth and Mandy Rodgers for helping this book find an audience. None of this would have been possible without the delightful team at Disney: Thank you to Holly Rice, Heather Knowles, Flannery Wiest, Shana Highfield, and Eugene Paraszczuk for your help, guidance, and invaluable knowledge. Additional appreciation is in order for the team at the Walt Disney Archives and the Animation Research Library for fact-checking the many details of the manuscript.

Thank you to Tim Burton, who gave me the gift of his time and who wrote an incredibly thoughtful foreword that makes this book that much better.

I'm deeply grateful to everyone who gave me their time to be interviewed for this book. Each of you made it more insightful and exciting. Thanks to Henry Selick, Danny Elfman, Catherine O'Hara, Rick Heinrichs, Deane Taylor, Caroline Thompson, Chris Sarandon, Paul Reubens, Denise Di Novi, Ken Page, Kat Alioshin, Todd Lookinland, Trey Thomas, Phil Lofaro, Allison Abbate, Richard Kraft, Laura Engel, Ian Nathan, Brian Volk Weiss, Dani Markman, Mark Hoppus, Jonathan Davis, Tim McIlrath, Tom Higgenson, Mike Retondo, Sonoko Ishioka, Terrell Gentry, Javier Garcia, Elise Barkan, George McClements, Ed La Bay, James Rendell, Leslie Kay, Rabab Al-Sharif, Rebecca Williams, Shea Ernshaw, Todd Martens, Lisa Morton, Katy Moore-Kozachik, Avery Smith, Kristen Vaughn-Smith, Sylvia Ward, TJ Neece, Valentina Ring, Ginny Philips, Julie Shepard, Renske Theuws, Margo Donis, Cassandra Franklin, Harli Hanson, and Jordan Baker.

Thank you to my parents, as always, and to my husband Dominic, who put up with me being on endless stream of Zoom interviews and didn't complain when I talked about this book constantly. And, finally, thank you to the fans of *Tim Burton's The Nightmare Before Christmas* for championing this film for thirty years. This book is for all of you.

ABOUT
THE AUTHOR

Emily Zemler is a freelance writer and journalist based in London. She is a frequent contributor to the *Los Angeles Times* and *Rolling Stone*, among other prestigious outlets. Emily is the co-author of *A Sick Life*, with TLC's Tionne "T-Boz" Watkins, and the author of *The Art and Making of Aladdin* and *Disney Princess: Beyond the Tiara*. Her favorite character in *Tim Burton's The Nightmare Before Christmas* is Zero.

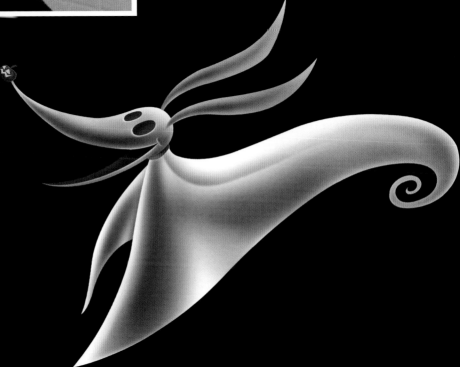

Jack's Journey from Page to Screen

December 23, 1832

Clement Clark Moore's iconic holiday verse "A Visit from St. Nicholas," more commonly known as "The Night Before Christmas," is published. It will later inspire Tim Burton to write a poem of his own, titled *The Nightmare Before Christmas*.

1912

The Cameraman's Revenge, an early example of stop-motion animation by filmmaker Ladislas Starevich, is released. Model maker and production designer Rick Heinrichs showed this short to the animators while making *Tim Burton's The Nightmare Before Christmas*.

1957

Dr. Seuss' *How the Grinch Stole Christmas!* is first published. The story of the misfit whose heart grows three sizes thanks to the holiday spirit also inspired Tim Burton's work on the poem that would later become *Tim Burton's The Nightmare Before Christmas*. "Dr. Seuss's books were perfect: right number of words, the right rhythm, great subversive stories," Burton said.

1958

The 7th Voyage of Sinbad is released, a film conceptualized by stop-motion master Ray Harryhausen. The story's fantastical creatures offered a starting point for Burton, who was also compelled by unlikely heroes and grotesque monsters.

1963

Jason and the Argonauts, a stop-motion film directed by Don Chaffey and brought to life by Ray Harryhausen, is released. It's also the first film Tim Burton remembers seeing in cinemas.

1964

Rudolph the Red-Nosed Reindeer, the Rankin/Bass Christmas classic, is released. It was filmed with a stop-motion animation process known as "Animagic" using small puppets. "Those crude stop-motion animation holiday things that were on year in, year out make an impact on you early and stay with you," Burton noted. "I had grown up with those and had a real feeling for them, and I think, without being too direct, the impulse was to do something like that."

1967

Mad Monster Party? is released. It was the first stop-motion animated feature musical film. Tim Burton has professed his admiration for the film, which he watched as a child.

1980s

Tim Burton graduates from the California Institute of the Arts and is hired as an animator and concept artist at Walt Disney Animation Studios. At Disney, he works on *The Fox and the Hound* (1981) and *The Black Cauldron* (1985), but the animation style doesn't quite fit his darker aesthetic. Burton continues to dream up ideas of his own.

1982

Vincent, Tim Burton's debut short film, is released. Burton wrote and directed the project, about a boy who wishes to be just like Vincent Price, for Disney, with the horror legend himself narrating.

1982

After a lifelong love of both Christmas and Halloween, Tim Burton writes a poem titled *The Nightmare Before Christmas*, his dark take on Clement Clark Moore's Christmas classic. His original intention was to publish it as a children's book, but every publisher he pitched it to ultimately passed on the project.

1990

Edward Scissorhands, directed by Tim Burton, is released. The film was written by Caroline Thompson, who would become instrumental in shaping the characters and narrative in *Tim Burton's The Nightmare Before Christmas*.

1990

The Walt Disney Company, owner of the rights to the *Nightmare* concept, agrees to let Tim Burton bring his vision to life on his own terms. Burton, who is signed on to direct *Batman Returns* at this time, taps Henry Selick to direct the film that would become *Tim Burton's The Nightmare Before Christmas*.

July 1991

Director Henry Selick and a crew of one hundred and twenty begin production on *Tim Burton's The Nightmare Before Christmas* at Skellington studio, a former warehouse in San Francisco's South of Market neighborhood.

August 5, 1991

The date on the first (and only) draft of the script for *Tim Burton's The Nightmare Before Christmas*, written by Caroline Thompson.

1992

Batman Returns, the follow-up to Tim Burton's popular *Batman* (1989), is released. Though directing *Batman Returns* meant Burton couldn't direct *Tim Burton's The Nightmare Before Christmas*, the two films share some inspirations: Sally's look in *Nightmare* is partly inspired by Michelle Pfeiffer's Catwoman in *Batman Returns*, while the super hero movie is set at Christmas, one of Burton's favorite holidays.

October 13, 1993

Tim Burton's The Nightmare Before Christmas is released. While the cast and crew were proud of their work, audiences didn't quite know what to make of the movie at first watch.

1996

James and the Giant Peach, directed by Henry Selick and adapted from Roald Dahl's 1961 children's novel of the same name, is released. The film combined stop-motion animation and live action, with the stop-motion scenes filmed at Skellington studios. Many of the crew members from *Tim Burton's The Nightmare Before Christmas* also worked on *James and the Giant Peach*, and Tim Burton and *Nightmare* producer Denise Di Novi returned to produce.

2000

Touchstone Home Video releases *Tim Burton's The Nightmare Before Christmas* as a special edition DVD with bonus features, including audio commentary from director Henry Selick, a making-of feature, and deleted scenes, allowing a wider audience to discover the film.

October 5, 2001

Haunted Mansion Holiday arrives at Disneyland! The annual overlay brings the unique characters, color palette, and style of *Tim Burton's The Nightmare Before Christmas* into the *Haunted Mansion* each fall and can be viewed until January. After the success of the attraction in California, a similar makeover was later brought to Tokyo Disneyland as *Haunted Mansion Holiday Nightmare*. Characters from *Nightmare* also appear at Mickey's Not-So-Scary Halloween Party at Walt Disney World in Florida, and Jack as Santa Claus often pops up during annual events at Walt Disney World's *Haunted Mansion* and Disneyland Paris's *Phantom Manor*.

Mid-2000s

Walt Disney Pictures, recognizing the immense fan base and the opportunities to grow the property, brings *Tim Burton's The Nightmare Before Christmas* back under their official umbrella.

2005

Tim Burton's Corpse Bride is released, in which a misfit protagonist falls in love with an unlikely leading lady. Tim Burton co-directed with Mike Johnson and many crew members from *Tim Burton's The Nightmare Before Christmas* returned—including Danny Elfman, who scored the movie.

October 20, 2006

Walt Disney Pictures converts *Tim Burton's The Nightmare Before Christmas* to Disney Digital 3D and re-releases the film in theaters, with special presentations at the Venice Film Festival and the London Film Festival.

September 30, 2008

Nightmare Revisited, an album of cover songs from *Tim Burton's The Nightmare Before Christmas*, is released by Walt Disney Records to commemorate the film's fifteenth anniversary. The album included a range of artists, from Amy Lee of Evanescence to Plain White T's and Korn.

2009

Coraline, directed by Henry Selick and based on a Neil Gaiman novella, is released. Like Jack stumbling upon the door to Christmas Town, Coraline also finds a door to another world.'

2012

Frankenweenie, directed by Tim Burton, is released. Burton revisited an idea from one of his earliest live-action shorts (*Frankenweenie*, 1984) to create this stop-motion horror-comedy, which became the first stop-motion film to be released in IMAX 3D, and was nominated for an Oscar, a Golden Globe, and a BAFTA. *Frankenweenie* shares the dark-yet-emotional tone of *Tim Burton's The Nightmare Before Christmas*.

2013

Danny Elfman performs live on stage (his first time singing publicly in eighteen years) at the Royal Albert Hall, closing a tribute to his musical collaborations with Tim Burton with a few songs from *Tim Burton's The Nightmare Before Christmas*.

2015

After the success at the Royal Albert Hall, Danny Elfman brings a full concert performance of *Tim Burton's The Nightmare Before Christmas* to Tokyo. The live concerts have since been performed in such notable locations as the Hollywood Bowl in Los Angeles and OVO Arena in London and have featured original cast members like Ken Page, Catherine O'Hara, and Paul Reubens, as well as guest stars like Billie Eilish and "Weird Al" Yankovic.

August 2, 2022

The young adult novel *Long Live the Pumpkin Queen*, written by Shea Ernshaw, is published. The novel, narrated by Sally, picks up after the events of *Nightmare* and details her adventures in the newly discovered Dream Town.

2022

Wendell & Wild, Henry Selick's most recent foray into stop motion animation, is released. The film was written by Selick and Jordan Peele, and also featured the work of a few of the animators who worked on *Tim Burton's The Nightmare Before Christmas*.

2023

Tim Burton's The Nightmare Before Christmas celebrates its thirtieth anniversary.

SOURCES

Print and Internet Sources

Adams, Tim. "Tim Burton: 'The love and life and death stuff was stewing from the start.'" *The Guardian*. 7 Oct. 2012.

Burton, Tim. *The Nightmare Before Christmas*. Disney Press, 1993.

Burton, Tim and Mark Salisbury. *Burton on Burton, 2nd Revised Edition*. Faber & Faber, 2006.

Ebert, Roger. "Tim Burton's The Nightmare Before Christmas." *Chicago Sun-Times*. 22 Oct. 1993.

Ernshaw, Shea. *Tim Burton's The Nightmare Before Christmas: Long Live the Pumpkin Queen*. Disney Press, 2022.

Foreman, Alison. 'Why 'The Nightmare Before Christmas' Is Really a Thanksgiving Movie." *Mashable*. 19 Nov. 2021. Web.

Goodman, William. "Evanescence's Amy Lee: 'It's Not All Sad.'" *SPIN*. 17 Oct. 2008. Web.

Kay, Leslie. *DisneyBound: Dress Disney and Make It Fashion*. Disney Editions, 2020.

Kozachik, Pete. *Tales from the Pumpkin King's Cameraman*. River Grove Books, 2021.

Laidlaw, Kim, Jody Revenson and Caroline Hall. *Tim Burton's The Nightmare Before Christmas: The Official Cookbook & Entertaining Guide Gift Set*. Insight Editions, 2021.

LeDonne, Rob. "'The Nightmare Before Christmas' at 25: Composer Danny Elfman on the Undying Classic." *Billboard*. 22 Oct. 2018.

McMahan, Alison. *The Films of Tim Burton: Animating Live Action in Contemporary Hollywood*. Continuum, 2005.

Milky, D.J. *Tim Burton's The Nightmare Before Christmas: Zero's Journey Graphic Novel Book One*. Disney Manga, 2018.

Nathan, Ian. *Tim Burton: The Iconic Filmmaker and His Work*. White Lion Publishing, 2019.

Neil, Zach. *The Nightmare Before Dinner: Recipes to Die For: The Beetle House Cookbook*. Race Point Publishing, 2018.

Page, Edwin. *Gothic Fantasy: The Films of Tim Burton*. Marion Boyars Publishers Ltd., 2006.

Thompson, Frank. *Tim Burton's The Nightmare Before Christmas: The Film, The Art, The Vision*. Disney Editions, 2009.

"Tim Burton on Ray Harryhausen, Stop-Motion and the Personal Touch of 'Frankenweenie.'" *UPROXX*. 4 Feb 2003. Web.

Travers, Peter. "Tim Burton's The Nightmare Before Christmas." *Rolling Stone*. 29 Oct. 1993.

Video and Audio Sources

Alioshin, Kat Miller and Todd Lookinland. "We Know Jack." Podcast.

Henry, Jason C. "Tim Burton's The Nightmare Before Christmas." *Prop Culture*. Netflix, 2020.

"Jack's Haunted Mansion Holiday Tour." *Tim Burton's The Nightmare Before Christmas.* Collector's Edition DVD. Walt Disney Studios, 2008.

Volk-Weiss, Brian. "Haunted Mansion." *Behind the Attraction*. Disney+, 2021.

Volk-Weiss, Brian. "The Nightmare Before Christmas." *The Holiday Movies That Made Us*. Netflix, 2020.

IMAGE CREDITS

Every effort has been made to trace copyright holders. If any unintentional omission has been made, Epic Ink, as an imprint of The Quarto Group, would be pleased to add appropriate acknowledgments in future editions.

Unless otherwise noted below, all images are copyright to The Walt Disney Company. © Disney Enterprises.

INDEX